Letters of
Samuel Rutherford

Letters of Samuel Rutherford

A Selection

THE BANNER OF TRUTH TRUST

THE BANNER OF TRUTH TRUST
3 Murrayfield Road, Edinburgh EH12 6EL
78b Chiltern Street, London WIM IPS
P.O. Box 652, Carlisle, Pa 17013, U.S.A.

First edition of Letters published 1664
This selection first published by the Banner of Truth Trust 197 3
© 1973 *The Banner of Truth Trust*
ISBN 85151 163 5

Printed in Great Britain by
Hunt Barnard Printing Ltd.,
Aylesbury, Bucks

CONTENTS

1/TO A CHRISTIAN GENTLEWOMAN   13
    [On the death of a daughter]
    Christ's sympathy with, and property in us
    Reasons for resignation
    23 April 1628

2/TO MARION M'NAUGHT   16
    Submission, perseverance and zeal recommended
    1630

3/TO LADY KENMURE   18
    God's inexplicable dealings with his people well-ordered
    Lack of ordinances
    Conformity to Christ
    Troubles of the Church
    Death of wife
    26 June 1630

4/TO MARION M'NAUGHT   20
    [In prospect of the Lord's Supper]
    Abundance in Jesus
    The restoration of the Jews
    Enemies of God
    7 May 1631

5/TO MARION M'NAUGHT   22
    The threatened introduction of the Service-Book
    Troubles of the Church
    Private wrongs
    2 June 1631

6/TO JOHN KENNEDY   25
    Deliverance from shipwreck
    Escape from threatened death
    Use of trials
    Remembrance of friends
    2 February 1632

7/TO LADY KENMURE   29
    A union for prayer recommended
    23 January 1634

8/TO LADY KENMURE   31
  [*On the death of Lord Kenmure*]
  Design of, and duties under affliction
  14 September 1634

9/TO MARION M'NAUGHT   33
  The prospect of exile in Aberdeen
  5 April 1636

10/TO LADY KENMURE   34
  [*On the eve of banishment to Aberdeen*]
  Rutherford's only regrets
  The cross unspeakably sweet
  Retrospect of his ministry
  28 July 1636

11/TO LADY CULROSS   37
  [*On the occasion of banishment to Aberdeen*]
  Challenges of conscience
  The cross no burden
  30 July 1636

12/TO ROBERT CUNNINGHAM   39
  Consolation to a brother in tribulation
  His own deprivation of ministry
  Christ worth suffering for
  4 August 1636

13/TO ALEXANDER GORDON   42
  Rutherford's feelings upon leaving Anwoth
  5 September 1636

14/TO LADY KENMURE   43
  Rutherford's enjoyment of Christ in Aberdeen
  A sight of Christ exceeds all reports
  Some ashamed of Christ and his people
  22 November 1636

15/TO HUGH M'KAIL   49
  Christ to be trusted amid trial
  22 November 1636

16/TO MARION M'NAUGHT   47
  Comfort under tribulations
  The prison a palace
  3 January 1637

17/TO JOHN GORDON, ELDER   48
  Win Christ at all hazards
  Christ's beauty
  A word to children
  1637

18/TO ROBERT BLAIR   52
  God's arrangements sometimes mysterious
  7 February 1637

19/TO ROBERT GORDON   55
   Visits of Christ
   Things which affliction teaches
   9 February 1637

20/TO LADY KENMURE   58
   None worthy but Christ
   'Anwoth is not heaven'
   1637

21/TO DAVID DICKSON   59
   God's dealings
   The bitter sweetened
   Notes on Scripture
   7 March 1637

22/TO ALEXANDER HENDERSON   61
   Sadness because Christ's Headship not set forth
   Christ's cause attended with crosses
   The believer seen of all
   9 March 1637

23/TO JOHN GORDON, YOUNGER   63
   Reasons for being earnest about the soul
   Resignation
   (Undated)

24/TO MARION M'NAUGHT   65
   Adherence to duty amidst opposition
   The power of Christ's love
   11 March 1637

25/TO WILLIAM LIVINGSTONE   66
   Counsel to a youth
   13 March 1637

26/TO THE LAIRD OF CARLETON   67
   Increasing sense of Christ's love
   Resignation
   Deadness to earth
   Temptations and infirmities
   14 March 1637

27/TO JOHN FLEMING   70
   Directions for Christian conduct
   15 March 1637

28/TO LADY BOYD   73
   Lessons learned in the school of adversity
   1 May 1637

29/TO JOHN STUART   76
   Commercial misfortunes
   Service-book
   Blessedness of trials
   1637

30/TO DAVID DICKSON   81
   Christ's infinite fulness
   1 May 1637

31/TO JOHN CLARK   83
   Marks of difference between Christians and reprobates
   (Undated)

32/TO EARLSTON, YOUNGER   84
   Dangers of youth
   Christ the best Physician
   Four remedies against doubting
   Breathing after Christ's honour
   16 June 1637

33/TO WILLIAM DALGLEISH   90
   Fragrance of the ministry
   Review of past and present situation, and of future prospects
   16 June 1637

34/TO JOHN STUART   94
   Hope for Scotland
   Self-submission
   Christ himself sought by faith
   Stability of salvation
   Christ's ways
   1637

35/TO EARLSTON, YOUNGER   97
   Sufferings
   Hope of final deliverance
   The believer in safe keeping
   Dependence on Christ for perseverance
   1637

36/TO WILLIAM GORDON   101
   Testimony to Christ's worth
   Marks of grace in conviction of sin and spiritual conflict
   1637

37/TO JOHN HENDERSON   104
   Practical hints
   (Undated)

38/TO ALEXANDER COLVILL   105
   Regrets for being silenced in ministry
   Longings for Christ
   23 June 1637

39/TO JAMES HAMILTON   106
    Suffering for Christ's Headship
    Christ's over-burdened Debtor
    7 July 1637

40/TO PARISHIONERS OF ANWOTH   109
    Protestation of care for their souls and for the glory of God
    Delight in his ministry and in his Lord
    Warnings against errors of the day
    Words to the backslider
    Intense admiration for Christ
    A loud call to all
    13 July 1637

41/TO LADY KILCONQUHAR   118
    The interests of the soul most urgent
    Folly of the world
    Christ altogether lovely
    Rutherford's pen fails to set forth Christ's unspeakable beauty
    8 August 1637

42/TO LORD CRAIGHALL   123
    Standing for Christ
    Danger from fear, and the falsity of men
    Christ's requitals for suffering
    Sin against the Holy Ghost
    10 August 1637

43/TO HUGH M'KAIL   126
    The Law
    This world is under Christ's control
    The security of believers
    5 September 1637

44/TO FULK ELLIS   128
    Friends in Ireland
    Difficulties in providence
    Sinning against light
    Constant need of Christ
    7 September 1637

45/TO JAMES LINDSAY   131
    Desertions and their use
    Prayers of reprobates
    How the Gospel affects the responsibility of reprobates
    7 September 1637

46/TO JAMES HAMILTON   135
    Christ's glory not affected by his people's weakness
    7 September 1637

47/TO LADY GAITGIRTH   137
    Christ an example in Cross-bearing
    The extent to which children should be loved
    Why saints die
    7 September 1637

48/TO MARION M'NAUGHT   139
    Prospects of his ministry
    Hopes
    Salutations
    7 September 1637

49/TO JAMES BAUTIE   140
    Spiritual difficulties resolved
    1637

50/TO THOMAS CORBET   147
    Godly counsels
    Following Christ
    1637

51/TO WILLIAM GLENDINNING   148
    Sweetness of trial
    Swiftness of time
    Prevalence of sin
    1637

52/TO MARION M'NAUGHT   150
    A Spring-tide of Christ's love
    22 November 1637

53/TO JOHN GORDON   152
    Heaven hard to be won
    Many come short of attaining
    Idol sins to be renounced
    Likeness to Christ
    1637

54/TO PARISHIONERS OF KILMALCOLM   155
    Spiritual sloth
    Advice to beginners
    A dead ministry
    Languor
    Obedience
    Want of Christ's felt presence
    Assurance important
    Prayer-meetings
    5 August 1639

55/TO ALEXANDER LEIGHTON   163
    Christs' prisoner in bonds at London
    Public blessings alleviate private sufferings
    Trials light when viewed in the light of Heaven
    Christ worthy of his people's sufferings
    22 November 1639

56/TO JAMES WILSON   166
   Advices to a doubting soul
   Mistakes about an interest in God's Love
   Temptation
   Perplexity about prayer
   Want of feeling
   8 January 1640

57/TO DAVID DICKSON   171
   [On the death of a son]
   God's sovereignty
   Discipline by affliction
   28 May 1640

58/TO LADY BOYD   173
   Proceedings of the Westminster Assembly
   25 May 1644

59/TO LADY KENMURE   175
   Westminster Assembly
   Religious sects
   4 March 1644

60/TO J.G.   176
   Depression in a cloudy day
   Darkness of the times
   Christ's infinite grace
   30 January 1646

61/TO WILLIAM GUTHRIE   178
   Depression under dark trials
   Dangers of compliance
   (Undated)

62/TO LADY RALSTON   179
   Duty of preferring to live rather than die
   Want of unity in the judgments of the godly
   October 1651

63/TO LADY KENMURE   183
   Trials
   Deadness of spirit
   Danger of false security
   26 May 1658

64/TO JAMES DURHAM   185
   [On his deathbed]
   Man's ways not God's ways
   15 June 1658

65/TO JAMES GUTHRIE, ROBERT TRAILL and other brethren
     imprisoned in Edinburgh Castle   186
   On suffering for Christ
   God's presence ever with his people
   Firmness and constancy required
   1660

66/TO MISTRESS CRAIG   188
   [On the death of her son]
   Nine reasons for resignation
   4 August 1660

67/TO JAMES GUTHRIE   190
   Steadfastness under persecution
   The blessedness of martyrdom
   15 February 1661

68/TO ROBERT CAMPBELL   192
   Steadfastness in protest against prelacy and popery
   (Undated)

69/TO BRETHERN IN ABERDEEN   194
   Sinful conformity and schismatic designs reproved
   (Undated)

BRIEF NOTES ON RUTHERFORD'S CORRESPONDENTS   199

AN OUTLINE OF RUTHERFORD'S LIFE   205

I/TO A CHRISTIAN GENTLEWOMAN

[On the death of a daughter]

Christ's sympathy with, and property in us
Reasons for resignation

Anwoth, 23 April 1628

Mistress:

My love in Christ remembered to you. I was indeed sorrowful
at my departure from you, especially since you were in such
heaviness after your daughter's death; yet I do persuade myself, you know that the weightiest end of the cross of Christ
that is laid upon you, lieth upon your strong Saviour. For
Isaiah saith that in all your afflictions he is afflicted [63. 9]. O
blessed Second, who suffereth with you! and glad may your
soul be, even to walk in the fiery furnace, with one like unto
the Son of man, who is also the Son of God. Courage up your
heart; when you tire, he will bear both you and your burden
[Psalm 55. 22]. Yet a little while, and you shall see the salvation of God.

Remember of what age your daughter was, and that just so
long was your lease of her. If she were eighteen, nineteen, or
twenty years old, I know not, but sure I am, seeing her term
was come, and your lease run out, you can no more justly
quarrel against your great Superior for taking his own, at his
just term-day, than a poor farmer can complain, that his
master taketh a portion of his own land to himself, when his
lease is expired. Good mistress, if you would not be content

that Christ would hold from you the heavenly inheritance, which is made yours by his death, will not that same Christ think hardly of you, if you refuse to give him your daughter willingly, who is a part of his inheritance and conquest? I pray the Lord to give you all your own, and to grace you with patience to give God his also. He is an ill debtor who payeth that which he hath borrowed with a grudge.

Indeed that long loan of such a good daughter, an heir of grace, a member of Christ (as I believe) deserveth more thanks at your creditor's hand, than that you should murmur, when he craveth but his own. I believe you would judge them to be but thankless neighbours who would pay you a sum of money after this manner.

But what! do you think her lost, when she is but sleeping in the bosom of the Almighty? Think her not absent who is in such a friend's house. Is she lost to you who is found to Christ? If she were with a dear friend, although you should never see her again, your care for her would be but small. Oh now, is she not with a dear friend, and gone higher, upon a certain hope that you shall in the resurrection see her again, when (be you sure) she shall neither be hectic nor consumed in body! You would be sorry either to be, or be esteemed an atheist; and yet not I, but the apostle [1 *Thess* 4. 13] thinketh those to be hopeless atheists who mourn excessively for the dead. But this is not a challenge on my part; I speak this, only fearing your weakness; for your daughter was a part of yourself; and therefore nature in you, being, as it were, cut and halved, will indeed be grieved; but you have to rejoice, that when a part of you is on earth, a great part of you is glorified in heaven.

Follow her, but envy her not; for indeed it is self-love in us that maketh us mourn for them that die in the Lord. Why? because for them we cannot mourn, since they are never happy till they be dead; therefore we mourn on our own private account. Take heed then, that in showing your affection in mourning for your daughter, you be not, out of self-affection, mourning for yourself.

Consider what the Lord is doing in it; your daughter is plucked out of the fire, and she resteth from her labours; and your Lord in that is trying you, and casting you in the fire. Go through all fires to your rest; and now remember, that the eye of God is upon the burning bush, and it is not consumed; and he is gladly content that such a weak woman as you should send Satan away, frustrated of his design. Now honour God, and shame the strong roaring lion, when you seem weakest.

Should such an one as you faint in the day of adversity? Call to mind the days of old; the Lord yet liveth; trust in him, although he should slay you. Faith is exceedingly charitable, and believeth no evil of God. Now is the Lord laying, in the one scale of the balance, your making conscience of submission to his gracious will; and in the other, your affection and love to your daughter. Which of the two will you then choose to satisfy? Be wise then; and, as I trust you love Christ better than a sinful woman, pass by your daughter, and kiss the Lord's rod. Men lop the branches off their trees round about, to the end they may grow up high and tall. The Lord hath this way lopped your branch in taking from you many children, to the end you should grow upward, like one of the Lord's cedars, setting your heart above, where Christ is at the right hand of the Father. What is next, but that your Lord cut down the stock, after he hath cut the branches?

Prepare yourself; you are nearer your daughter this day than you were yesterday. While you prodigally spend time in mourning for her, you are speedily posting after her. Run your race with patience; let God have his own, and ask of him, instead of your daughter, whom he hath taken from you, the daughter of faith, which is patience; and in patience possess your soul. Lift up your head; you do not know how near your redemption doth draw. Thus, recommending you to the

Lord, who is able to establish you, I rest.

Your loving and affectionate friend in the Lord Jesus,

S.R.

2/TO MARION M'NAUGHT

Submission, perseverance, and zeal recommended

Anwoth, undated [probably 1630]

Well-beloved and dear Sister in Christ:

I could not get an answer written to your letter till now, in respect of my wife's disease; and she is yet mightily pained. I hope that all shall end in God's mercy. I know that an afflicted life looks very like the way that leads to the kingdom; for the Apostle hath drawn the line and the King's market-way, 'through much tribulation, to the kingdom' [*Acts* 14. 22; 1 *Thess* 3. 4]. The Lord grant us the whole armour of God!

You write to me concerning your people's disposition, how that their hearts are inclined toward the man you know, and whom you desire most earnestly yourself. He would most gladly have the Lord's call for transplantation; for he knows that all God's plants, set by his own hand, thrive well; and if the work be of God, he can make a stepping-stone of the devil himself for setting forward the work. For yourself, I would advise you to ask of God a submissive heart. Your reward shall be with the Lord, although the people be not gathered (as the prophet speaks); and suppose the Word do not prosper, God shall account you 'a repairer of the breaches'. And take Christ caution, you shall not lose your reward. Hold your grip fast.

If you knew the mind of the glorified in heaven, they think

heaven come to their hand at an easy market, when they have got it for threescore or fourscore years' wrestling with God. When you are come thither you shall think, 'All I did, in respect of my rich reward, now enjoyed of free grace, was too little'. Now then, for the love of the Prince of your salvation, who is standing at the end of your way, holding up in his hand the prize and the garland to the race-runners, Forward, forward! faint not! Take as many to heaven with you as you are able to draw. The more you draw with you, you shall be the welcomer yourself. Be no niggard or sparing churl of the grace of God; and employ all your endeavours for establishing an honest ministry in your town, now when you have so few to speak a good word for you.

I have many a grieved heart daily in my calling. I would be undone if I had not access to the King's chamber of presence, to show him all the business. The devil rages, and is mad to see the water drawn from his own mill; but would to God we could be the Lord's instruments to build the Son of God's house.

Pray for me. If the Lord furnish not new timber from Lebanon to build the house, the work will cease. I look to him, who hath begun well with me. I have his handwrite, he will not change. Your daughter is well, and longs for a Bible. The Lord establish you in peace. The Lord Jesus be with your spirit.

3/TO LADY KENMURE

God's inexplicable dealings with his people well-ordered
Lack of ordinances
Conformity to Christ
Troubles of the Church
Death of wife

Anwoth, 26 June 1630

Madam:

Grace, mercy and peace be multiplied upon you. I received your Ladyship's letter, in the which I perceive your case in this world savoureth of worship and communion with the Son of God, in his sufferings. You cannot, you must not have a more pleasant or more easy condition here, than he had, who 'through afflictions was made perfect' [*Heb* 2. 10]. We may indeed think, Cannot God bring us to heaven with ease and prosperity? Who doubteth but he can? But his infinite wisdom thinketh and decreeth the contrary; and though we cannot see a reason for it, yet he hath a most just reason. We never with our eyes saw our own soul, yet we have a soul; we see many rivers, but we know not their first spring and original fountain, yet they have a beginning.

Madam, when you are come to the other side of the water, and have set down your foot on the shore of glorious eternity, and look back again to the waters and to your wearisome journey, and shall see in that clear glass of endless glory nearer to the bottom of God's wisdom, you shall then be forced to say, 'If God had done otherwise with me than he hath done, I had never come to the enjoying of this crown of glory'. It is your part now to believe, and suffer, and hope, and wait on: for I protest in the presence of that all-discerning eye who knoweth what I write and what I think, that I would not want the sweet experience of the consolations of God for all the bitterness of affliction; nay, whether God come to his children with a rod or a crown, if he come himself with it, it is well. Welcome, welcome Jesus, what way soever thou come, if we can get a sight of thee. And sure I am, it is better to be sick, providing Christ come to the bed-side, and draw aside the curtains, and say 'Courage, I am thy salvation,' than to enjoy health, being lusty and strong, and never to be visited of God.

Worthy and dear lady, in the strength of Christ, fight and overcome. You are now alone, but you may have, for the seeking, three always in your company, the Father, Son and Holy Spirit. I trust they are near you. You are now deprived of the comfort of a lively ministry; so were Israel in their captivity; yet hear God's promise to them: 'Therefore say, Thus saith the Lord God, although I have cast them far off among the heathen, and although I have scattered them among the countries, yet will I be to them as a little sanctuary in the countries where they shall come' [*Ezek* 11. 16]. Behold a sanctuary! for a sanctuary, God himself, in the place and room of the temple of Jerusalem: I trust in God, that carrying this temple about with you, you shall see Jehovah's beauty in his house.

We are in great fears of a great and fearful trial to come upon the kirk of God; for these, who would build their houses and nests upon the ashes of mourning Jerusalem, have drawn our king[1] upon hard and dangerous conclusions, against such as are termed puritans, for the rooting of them out. Our prelates assure us that for such as will not conform, there is nothing but imprisonment and deprivation. The spouse of Jesus will ever be in the fire; but I trust in my God she shall not consume, because of the good-will of him who dwelleth in the bush, for he dwelleth in it with good-will. All sorts of crying sins without controlment abound in our land; the glory of the Lord is departing from Israel, and the Lord is

[1] Charles I: the reference is to the episcopal dislike of stalwart presbyterians.

looking back over his shoulder, to see if any will say, 'Lord, tarry,' and no man requesteth him to stay.

For myself, I have daily griefs, through the disobedience unto and contempt of the Word of God. I was summoned before the High Commission[1] by a profligate person in this parish, convicted of incest. In the business, Mr Alexander Colvill (for respect to your Ladyship) was my great friend, and wrote a most kind letter to me; the Lord give him mercy in that day.

My wife now, after a long disease and torment, for the space of a year and a month, is departed this life; the Lord hath done it, blessed be his name. I have been diseased of a fever tertian for the space of thirteen weeks, and am yet in that sickness, so that I preach but once on the sabbath with great difficulty. I am not able either to visit or examine the congregation. The Lord Jesus be with your spirit.

4/TO MARION M'NAUGHT

[*In prospect of the Lord's Supper*]

Abundance in Jesus
The restoration of the Jews
Enemies of God

Anwoth, 7 May 1631

Well-beloved in the Lord:

You are not unacquainted with the day of our Communion. I entreat, therefore, the aid of your prayers for that great work, which is one of our feast days, wherein our well-beloved Jesus rejoiceth and is merry with his friends.

Good cause have we to wonder at his love, since the day

[1] The Court of High Commission was set up in Scotland in 1610.

of his death was such a sorrowful day to him, even the day when his mother, the kirk, crowned him with thorns, and he had many against him, and appeared his lone in the fields against them all; yet he delights with us to remember that day. Let us love him, and be glad and rejoice in his salvation. I am confident that you shall see the Son of God that day, and I dare in his name invite you to his banquet. Many a time you have been well entertained in his house; and he changes not upon his friends, nor chides them for too great kindness.

Yet I speak not this to make you leave off to pray for me, who have nothing of myself, but in so far as daily I receive from him who is made of his Father a running-over fountain, at which I and others may come with thirsty souls and fill our vessels. Long hath this well been standing open to us. Lord Jesus, lock it not up again upon us. I am sorry for our desolate kirk; yet I dare not but trust, so long as there be any of God's lost money here, he shall not blow out the candle. The Lord make fair candlesticks in his house, and remove the blind lights.

I have been this time bypast thinking much of the incoming of the kirk of the Jews. Pray for them. When they were in their Lord's house, at their Father's elbow, they were longing for the incoming of their little sister, the kirk of the Gentiles. They said to their Lord, 'We have a little sister and she hath no breasts; what shall we do for our sister in the day when she shall be spoken for?' [*Cant* 8. 8]. Let us give them a meeting. What shall we do for our elder sister, the Jews? Lord Jesus, give them breasts. That were a glad day to see us and them both sit down to one table, and Christ at the head of the table. Then would our Lord come shortly with his fair guard to hold his great court.

Dear sister, be patient for the Lord's sake under the wrongs that you suffer of the wicked. Your Lord shall make you see your desire on your enemies. Some of them shall be cut off: 'they shall shake off their unripe grapes as the vine, and cast

off their flower as the olive' [*Job* 15. 33]. God shall make them
like unripe sour grapes, shaken off the tree with the blast of
God's wrath; and therefore pity them and pray for them.
Others of them must remain to exercise you. God hath said
of them, 'Let the tares grow up until harvest' [*Matt* 13. 30].
It proves you to be your Lord's wheat. Be patient; Christ
went to heaven with many a wrong. His visage and countenance was all marred more than the sons of men. You may not
be above your Master; many a black stroke received innocent
Jesus, and he received no mends, but referred them all to the
great court-day when all things shall be righted.

I desire to hear from you within a day or two, if Mr Robert
remains in his purpose to come and help us. God shall give
you joy of your children. I pray for them by their names. I
bless you from our Lord, your husband and children. Grace,
grace and mercy be multiplied upon you.

5/TO MARION M'NAUGHT

> The threatened introduction of the Service-Book
> Troubles of the Church
> Private wrongs

Anwoth, 2 June 1631

Well-beloved Sister,

My love in Christ remembered. I have received a letter from
Edinburgh, certainly informing me that the English service,
and the organs, and King James' Psalms, are to be imposed
upon our kirk, and that the bishops are dealing for a general
assembly. A.R. hath confirmed the news also, and says he
spoke with Sir William Alexander,[1] who is to come down

[1] Afterwards Earl of Stirling.

with his prince's warrant for that effect. I am desired in the received letter to acquaint the best-affected about me with that storm; therefore I entreat you, and charge you in the Lord's name, pray. But do not communicate this to any till I see you. My heart is broken at the remembrance of it, and it was my fear, and answereth to my last letter except one, that I wrote unto you.

Dearly beloved, be not casten down, but let us, as our Lord's doves, take us to our wings (for other armour we have none) and flee into the hole of the rock. It is true, A.R. says, the worthiest men in England are banished and silenced, about the number of sixteen or seventeen choice Gospel preachers, and the persecution is already begun.[1] Howbeit I do not write this unto you with a dry face, yet I am confident in the Lord's strength, Christ and his side shall overcome; and you shall be assured. The kirk were not a kirk if it were not so.

As our dear Husband, in wooing his kirk, received many a black stroke, so his bride, in wooing him, gets many blows, and in this wooing there are strokes upon both sides. Let it be so. The devil will not make the marriage go back, neither can he tear the contract; the end shall be mercy. Yet notwithstanding of all this, we have no warrant of God to leave off all lawful means. I have been writing unto you the counsels and draughts[2] of men against the kirk; but they know not, as Micah says, the counsel of Jehovah. The great men of the world may make ready the fiery furnace for Zion, but trow ye that they can cause the fire to burn? No! He that made the fire, I trust, shall not say amen to their decreets.[3] I trust in my Lord, that God hath not subscribed their bill, and their conclusions have not yet passed our great King's seal. Therefore, if ye think good, address yourself first to the Lord, and then to A.R., anent the business that you know.

---

[1]This seems to refer to the silencing of Puritans by Laud, then Bishop of London (Archbishop of Canterbury from 1633). He became Charles I's chief adviser in religious matters.   [2] Plans.   [3] Judicial sentences.

I am most unkindly handled by the presbytery; and (as if I had been a stranger and not a member of that seat, to sit in judgment with them) I was summoned by their order as a witness against B.A. But they have got no advantage in that matter. Other particulars you shall hear, God willing, at meeting.

Anent the matter betwixt you and I.E., I remember it to God. I entreat you in the Lord, be submissive to his will; for the higher that their pride mounts up, they are the nearer to a fall. The Lord will more and more discover that man. Let your husband, in all matters of judgment, take Christ's part, for the defence of the poor and needy and the oppressed, for the maintenance of equity and justice in the town. And take you no fear. He shall take your part, and then you are strong enough. What! Howbeit you receive indignities for your Lord's sake, let it be so. When he shall put his holy hand up to your face in heaven, and dry your face, and wipe the tears from your eyes, judge if you will not have cause then to rejoice. Anent other particulars, if you would speak with me, appoint any of the first three days of the next week in Carletoun,[1] when Carletoun is at home, and acquaint me with your desires. And remember me to God, and my dearest affection to your husband; and for Zion's sake hold not your peace. The grace of our Lord Jesus Christ be with you, and your husband and children.

---

[1] Carleton, in Galloway, not far from Anwoth.

6/TO JOHN KENNEDY

Deliverance from shipwreck
Escape from threatened death
Use of trials
Remembrance of friends

Anwoth, 2 February 1632

My loving and most affectionate brother in Christ:

I salute you with grace, mercy and peace from God our Father, and from our Lord Jesus Christ. I heard with grief of your great danger of perishing by the sea, but of your merciful deliverance with joy. Sure I am, brother, Satan will leave no stone unrolled, as the proverb is, to roll you off your Rock, or at least to shake and unsettle you: for at the same time, the mouths of wicked men were opened in hard speeches against you, by land, and the prince of the power of the air was angry with you, by sea. See then how much you are obliged to that malicious murderer, who would beat you with two rods at one time. But, blessed be God, his arm is short: if the sea and winds would have obeyed him, you had never come to land. Thank your God, who saith, 'I have the keys of hell and of death' [*Rev* 1. 18]. 'I kill and make alive' [*Deut* 32. 39]. 'The Lord bringeth down to the grave, and bringeth up' [1 *Sam* 2. 6] If Satan were jailer, and had the keys of death and of the grave, they should be stored with more prisoners. You were knocking at these black gates, and found the doors shut; and we do all welcome you back again.

I trust you know it is not for nothing that you are sent to us again. The Lord knew you had forgotten something that was necessary for your journey; that your armour was not as yet thick enough against the stroke of death. Now, in the strength of Jesus, dispatch your business; that debt is not forgiven, but deferred; death hath not bidden you farewell, but hath only left you for a short season. End your journey ere the night come upon you; have all in readiness against the time that you must fall through that black and impetuous Jordan; and Jesus, Jesus, who knoweth both those depths and the rocks and all the coasts, be your Pilot. The last tide will not wait for you one moment; if you forget anything, when your sea is full, and your foot in that ship, there is no returning again to fetch it. What you do amiss in your life today, you may amend tomorrow; for as many suns as God maketh to arise upon you, you have as many new lives; but you can die but once; and if you mar that business, you cannot come back to mend that piece of work again; no man sinneth twice in dying ill; as we die but once, so we die but ill or well once. You see how the number of your months is written in God's book; and as one of the Lord's hirelings, you must work till the shadow of the evening come upon you, and you shall run out your glass even to the last grain of sand. Fulfil your course with joy; for we take nothing to the grave with us, but a good or evil conscience. And although the sky clear after this storm, yet clouds will engender another.

You contracted with Christ, I hope, when first you began to follow him, that you would bear his cross. Fulfil your part of the contract with patience, and break not to Jesus Christ. Be honest, brother, in your bargaining with him; for who knoweth better how to bring up children than our God? For (to lay aside his knowledge, which there is no searching out) he hath been practised in bringing up his heirs these five thousand years, and his children are all well brought up, and many of them are honest men now at home, up in their own house in heaven, and are entered heirs to their Father's inheritance.

Now, the form of his bringing up was by chastisements, scourging, correcting, nurturing. See if he maketh exception of any of his children [Rev 3.19; Heb 12.7, 8]. No! His eldest Son and his Heir, Jesus, is not excepted [Heb 2. 10]. Suffer we must;

ere we were born, God decreed it; and it is easier to complain of his decree than to change it. It is true, terrors of conscience cast us down; and yet without terrors of conscience we cannot be raised up again; fears and doubtings shake us; and yet without fear and doubtings we should soon sleep, and lose our hold of Christ. Tribulation and temptations will almost loose us at the root; and yet without tribulations and temptations we can now no more grow than herbs or corn without rain. Sin and Satan and the world will say, and cry in our ear, that we have a hard reckoning to make in judgment; and yet none of these three, except they lie, dare say in our face that our sin can change the tenor of the new covenant.

Forward then, dear brother, and lose not your grips. Hold fast the truth; for the world sells not one drachm-weight of God's truth, especially now when most men measure truth by time, like young seamen setting their compass by a cloud: for now time is father and mother to truth, in the thoughts and practices of our evil time. The God of truth establish us; for, alas! now there are none to comfort the prisoners of hope, and the mourners in Zion. We can do little except pray and mourn for Joseph in the stocks. And let their tongue cleave to the roof of their mouth who forget Jerusalem now in her day: and the Lord remember Edom, and render to him as he hath done to us.

Now, brother, I will not weary you; but I entreat you, remember my dearest love to Mr David Dickson, with whom I have small acquaintance; yet I bless the Lord, I know he both prayeth and doeth for our dying kirk. Remember my dearest love to John Stuart, whom I love in Christ; and show him from me that I do always remember him, and hope for a meeting. The Lord Jesus establish him more and more, though he be already a strong man in Christ. Remember my heartiest affection in Christ to William Rodger, whom I also remember to God. I wish the first news I hear of him and you, and all that love our common Saviour in those bounds, may be, that ye are so knit and linked and kindly fastened in love with the Son of God, that ye may say, 'Now, if we would never so fain escape out of Christ's hands, yet love hath so bound us that we cannot get our hands free again; he hath so ravished our hearts, that there is no loosing of his grips; the chains of his soul-ravishing love are so strong that neither the grave nor death will break them.'

I hope, brother, yea, I doubt not of it, that you lay me, and my first entry to the Lord's vineyard, and my flock, before him who hath put me in his work. As the Lord knoweth, since first I saw you, I have been mindful of you. Marion M'Naught doth remember most heartily her love to you, and to John Stuart. Blessed be the Lord, that in God's mercy I found in this country such a woman, to whom Jesus is dearer than her own heart, when there be so many that cast Christ over their shoulder. Good brother, call to mind the memory of your worthy father, now asleep in Christ; and, as his custom was, pray continually, and wrestle for the life of a dying breathless kirk. And desire John Stuart not to forget poor Zion; she hath few friends, and few to speak one good word for her. Now I commend you, your whole soul and body and spirit, to Jesus Christ and his keeping, hoping you will live and die, stand and fall, with the cause of our Master, Jesus. The Lord Jesus himself be with your spirit.

7/TO LADY KENMURE

A union for prayer recommended

Anwoth, 23 January 1634

Madam:

Having received a letter from some of the worthiest of the ministry in this kingdom, the contents whereof I am desired to communicate to such professors in these parts as I know love the beauty of Zion, and are afflicted to see the Lord's vineyard trodden under foot by the wild boars out of the wood who lay it waste, I could not but also desire your Ladyship's help to join with the rest, desiring you to impart it to my Lord your husband, and if you think it needful, I shall write to his Lordship, as Mr G.G. shall advertise[1] me.

Know, therefore, that the best affected of the ministry have thought it convenient and necessary, at such a time as this, that all who love the truth should join their prayers together, and cry to God with humiliation and fasting. The times which are agreed upon are the two first Sabbaths of February next, and the six days intervening betwixt these Sabbaths, as they may conveniently be had, and the first Sabbath of every quarter. And the causes as they are written to me are these:

1. Besides the distresses of the Reformed churches abroad, the many reigning sins of uncleanness, ungodliness and unrighteousness in this land, the present judgments on the land, and many more hanging over us, whereof few are sensible, or yet know the right and true cause of them.

2. The lamentable and pitiful estate of a glorious church (in so short a time, against so many bonds), in doctrine, sacrament, and discipline, so sore persecuted in the persons

[1]Notify, inform.

of faithful pastors and professors, and the door of God's house kept so straight by bastard porters, insomuch that worthy instruments, able for the work, are held at the door, the rulers having turned over religion into policy, and the multitude ready to receive any religion that shall be enjoined by authority.

3. In our humiliation, besides that we are under a necessity of deprecating God's wrath, and vowing to God sincerely new obedience, the weakness, coldness, silence, and lukewarmness of some of the best of the ministry, and the deadness of professors, who have suffered the truth both secretly to be stolen away, and openly to be plucked from us, would be confessed.

4. Atheism, idolatry, profanity, and vanity should be confessed; our king's heart recommended to God; and God intreated that he would stir up the nobles and the people to turn from their evil ways.

Thus, Madam, hoping that your Ladyship will join with others that such a work be not slighted at such a necessary time when our kirk is at the overturning, I will promise to myself your help, as the Lord in secrecy and prudence shall enable you, that your Ladyship may rejoice with the Lord's people when deliverance shall come; for true and sincere humiliation come always speed with God. And when authority, king, court, and churchmen oppose the truth, what other armour have we but prayer and faith? whereby, if we wrestle with him, there is ground to hope that those who would remove the burdensome stone [*Zech* 12. 3] out of its place shall but hurt their back, and the stone shall not be moved, at least not removed.

Grace, grace be with you, from him who hath called you to the inheritance of the saints in light.

8/TO LADY KENMURE

[*On the death of Lord Kenmure*]
Design of, and duties under affliction

Anwoth, 14 September 1634

My very noble and worthy Lady:

Often I call to mind the comforts that I myself, a poor friend-less stranger, received from your Ladyship here, in a strange part of the country, when my Lord took from me the delight of mine eyes as the word speaketh [*Ezek* 24. 16], which wound is not yet fully healed and cured. I trust your Lord will remember that, and give you comfort now, at such a time as this, wherein your dearest Lord hath made you a widow, that you may be a free woman for Christ. Seeing, among all crosses spoken of in our Lord's word, this giveth you a particular right to make God your husband (which was not so yours while your husband was alive), read God's mercy out of this visitation; and albeit I must, out of some experience, say, the mourning for the husband of your youth be, by God's own mouth, the heaviest worldly sorrow [*Joel* 1. 8], and though this be the weightiest burden that ever lay upon your back, yet you know (when the fields are emptied, and your husband now asleep in the Lord), if you shall wait upon him who hideth his face for a while, that it lieth upon God's honour and truth to fill the field, and to be a husband to the widow.

See and consider, then, what you have lost, and how little it is. Therefore, madam, let me intreat you, in the bowels of Christ Jesus, and by the comforts of his Spirit, and your appearance before him, let God and men and angels now see what is in you. The Lord hath pierced the vessel; it will be known whether there be in it wine or water. Let your faith and patience be seen, that it may be known that your only beloved, first and last, hath been Christ. And, therefore, now, were your whole love upon him, he alone is a suitable object for your love and all the affections of your soul. God hath dried up one channel of your love by the removal of your husband; let now that speat[1] run upon Christ. Your Lord and lover hath graciously taken your husband's name, and your name, out of the summones that are raised at the instance of the terrible sin-avenging Judge of the world against the house of Kenmure. And I dare say that God's hammering of you from your youth is only to make you a fair-carved stone in the high upper temple of the New Jerusalem.

Your Lord never thought this world's vain painted glory a gift worthy of you; and therefore would not bestow it on you, because he is to provide you with a better portion. Let the moveables go, the inheritance is yours. You are a child of the house, and joy is laid up for you; it is long in coming, but not the worse for that. I am now expecting to see, and that with joy and comfort, that which I hoped of you, since I knew you fully; even that you have laid such strength upon the Holy One of Israel that you defy troubles; and that your soul is a castle that may be besieged but cannot be taken.

What have you to do here? This world never looked like a friend upon you; you owe it little love; it looked ever sour-like upon you: howbeit you should woo it, it will not match with you; and, therefore, never seek warm fire under cold ice. This is not a field where your happiness groweth; it is up above, where there are 'a great multitude which no man can number, of all nations and kindreds, and people, and tongues, standing before the throne, and before the Lamb, clothed with white robes, and palms in their hands' [*Rev* 7. 9]. What you could never get here you shall find there. And withal, consider how, in all these trials (and truly they have been many),

[1]Flood, overflowing stream.

your Lord hath been loosing you at the root from perishing things, and hunting after you to grip your soul. Madam, for the Son of God's sake, let him not miss his grip, but stay and abide in the love of God, as Jude saith [ver. 21].

Now, madam, I hope your Ladyship will take these lines in good part; and wherein I have fallen short and failed to your Ladyship, in not evidencing what I was obliged to your more than undeserved love and respect, I request for a full pardon for it. Again, my dear and noble lady, let me beseech you to lift your head, for the day of your redemption draweth near: and, remember, that star which shined in Galloway is now shining in another world. Now I pray that God may answer in his own style to your soul; and that he may be to you the God of all consolations.

9/TO MARION M'NAUGHT

The prospect of exile in Aberdeen

Edinburgh, 5 April 1636

Honoured and dearest in the Lord:

Grace, mercy and peace be to you. I am well and my soul prospereth. I find Christ with me. I burden no man, I want nothing, no face looketh on me but it laugheth on me. Sweet, sweet is the Lord's cross. I overcome my heaviness. My Bridegroom's love-blinks fatten my weary soul. I soon go to my King's palace at Aberdeen. Tongue and pen and wit cannot express my joy.

Remember my love to Jean Gordon, to my sister, Jean Brown, to Grizel, to your husband. Thus in haste. Grace be with you.

Yours in his only, only Lord Jesus,

S.R.

P.S. My charge is to you to believe, rejoice, sing and triumph.
Christ has said to me, Mercy, mercy, grace and peace for
Marion M'Naught.

10/TO LADY KENMURE

[*On the eve of banishment to Aberdeen*]

His only regrets
The cross unspeakably sweet
Retrospect of his ministry

Edinburgh, 28 July 1636

Noble and elect Lady:

That honour that I have prayed for these sixteen years, with
submission to my Lord's will, my kind Lord hath now
bestowed upon me, even to suffer for my royal and princely
Lord Jesus and for his kingly crown and the freedom of his
kingdom that his Father hath given him. The forbidden lords
have sentenced me with deprivation, and confinement within
the town of Aberdeen. I am charged in the King's name to
enter against the 20th day of August next, and there to
remain during the King's pleasure, as they have given it out.

Howbeit Christ's green cross, newly laid upon me, be
somewhat heavy, while I call to mind the many fair days
sweet and comfortable to my soul and to the souls of many
others, and how young ones in Christ are plucked from my
breast, and the inheritance of God laid waste; yet that sweet-
smelled and perfumed cross of Christ is accompanied with
sweet refreshments, with the kisses of a King, with the joy
of the Holy Ghost, with faith that the Lord hears the sighing

of a prisoner, with undoubted hope (as sure as my Lord liveth) after this night to see daylight, and Christ's sky to clear up again upon me and his poor kirk; and that in a strange land, among strange faces, he will give favour in the eyes of men to his poor oppressed servant, who cannot but love that lovely One, that princely One, Jesus, the Comforter of his soul.

All would be well if I were free of old challenges for guiltiness, and for neglect in my calling, and for speaking too little for my Well-beloved's crown, honour and kingdom. O for a day in the assembly of the saints to advocate for King Jesus! If my Lord also go on now to quarrels I die, I cannot endure it. But I look for peace from him, because he knoweth I am able to bear men's feud, but I cannot bear his feud. This is my only exercise, that I fear I have done little good in my ministry. But I dare not but say I loved the children of the wedding-chamber, and prayed for and desired the thriving of the marriage and coming of his kingdom.

I apprehend no less than a judgment upon Galloway, and that the Lord shall visit this whole nation for the quarrel of the Covenant. But what can be laid upon me, or any the like of me, is too light for Christ. Christ is able to bear more, and would bear death and burning quick,[1] in his quick[1] servants, even for this honourable cause that I now suffer for. Yet for all my complaints (and he knoweth that I dare not now dissemble) he was never sweeter and kinder than he is now. One kiss now is sweeter than ten long since; sweet, sweet is his cross; light, light and easy is his yoke. O what a sweet step were it up to my Father's house through ten deaths, for the truth and cause of that unknown, and so not half well loved, Plant of Renown, the Man called the Branch, the Chief among ten thousands, the fairest among the sons of men! O what unseen joys, how many heart-burnings of love,

[1] Living.

are in the 'remnants of the sufferings of Christ!' [*Col* 1. 24].

My dear worthy lady, I give it to your Ladyship, under my own hand, my heart writing as well as my hand – welcome welcome, sweet, sweet and glorious cross of Christ; welcome, sweet Jesus, with thy light cross. Thou hast now gained and gotten all my love from me; keep what thou hast gotten! Only woe, woe is me, for my bereft flock, for the lambs of Jesus, that I fear shall be fed with dry breasts. But I spare now. Madam, I dare not promise to see your Ladyship, because of the little time I have allotted me; and I purpose to obey the King, who hath power of my body; and rebellion to kings is unbeseeming Christ's ministers. Be pleased to acquaint my Lady Mar with my case. I will look that your Ladyship and that good lady will be mindful to God of the Lord's prisoner, not for my cause, but for the Gospel's sake. Madam, bind me more, if more can be, to your Ladyship, and write thanks to your brother, my Lord of Lorn, for what he hath done for me, a poor unknown stranger to his Lordship. I shall pray for him and his house while I live. It is his honour to open his mouth in the streets, for his wronged and oppressed Master, Christ Jesus.

Now, madam, commending your Ladyship and the sweet child to the tender mercies of mine own Lord Jesus, and his good-will who dwelt in the bush.

I am yours in his own sweetest Lord Jesus,

S.R.

11/TO LADY CULROSS

[*On the occasion of his banishment to Aberdeen*]

Challenges of conscience
The cross no burden

Edinburgh, 30 July 1636

Madam:

Your letter came in due time to me, now a prisoner of Christ, and in bonds for the gospel. I am sentenced with deprivation, and confinement within the town of Aberdeen; but O, my guiltiness, the follies of my youth, the neglects in my calling, and especially in not speaking more for the kingdom, crown and sceptre of my royal and princely King Jesus, do so stare me in the face, that I apprehend anger in that which is a crown of rejoicing to the dear saints of God! This, before my appearance (which was three several days) did trouble me, and burdeneth me more now. Howbeit Christ, and, in him, God reconciled, met me with open arms, and trysted me, precisely at the entry of the door of the Chancellor's hall, and assisted me so to answer, as that the advantage is not theirs but Christ's.

Alas! that is no cause of wondering that I am thus borne down with challenges; for the world hath mistaken me, and no man knoweth what guiltiness is in me so well as these two (who keep my eyes now waking and my heart heavy); I mean, my heart and conscience, and my Lord, who is greater than my heart. Show your brother that I desire him, while he is on the watch-tower, to plead with his mother; and to plead with this land, and spare not to cry for my sweet Lord Jesus' fair crown.

If I were free of challenges and a High Commission within my soul, I would not give a straw to go to my Father's house, through ten deaths, for the truth and cause of my lovely, lovely One, Jesus; but I walk in heaviness now. If you love me, and Christ in me, my dear lady, pray, pray for this only, that bygones betwixt my Lord and me may be bygones; and that he would pass from the summons of his High Commission, and seek nothing from me but what he will do for me and work in me. If your Ladyship knew me as I do myself, you would say 'Poor soul, no marvel'. It is not my apprehension that createth this cross to me; it is too real, and hath sad and certain grounds. But I will not believe that God will take this advantage of me when my back is at the wall. He who forbiddeth to add affliction to affliction, will he do it himself? Why should he pursue a dry leaf and stubble? Desire him to spare me now. Also the memory of the fair feast-days that Christ and I had in his banqueting-house, and of the scattered flock once committed to me, and now taken off my hand by himself, because I was not so faithful in the end as I was in the first two years of my entry, when sleep departed from my eyes because my soul was taken up with a care for Christ's lambs – even these add sorrow to my sorrow.

Now my Lord hath only given me this to say, and I write it under mine own hand (be you the Lord's servant's witness), welcome, welcome, sweet, sweet cross of Christ; welcome, fair, fair, lovely, royal King, with thine own cross; let us all three go to heaven together. Neither care I much to go from the south of Scotland to the north, and to be Christ's prisoner amongst uncouth faces; a place of this kingdom which I have little reason to be in love with. I know Christ shall make Aberdeen my garden of delights. I am fully persuaded that Scotland shall eat Ezekiel's book, that is written within and without, 'lamentation, and mourning, and woe' [*Ezek* 2. 10]; but the saints shall get a drink of the well that goeth through the streets of the New Jerusalem, to put it down. Thus, hoping you will think upon the poor prisoner of Christ, I pray, grace, grace be with you.

12/TO ROBERT CUNNINGHAM

Consolation to a brother in tribulation
His own deprivation of ministry
Christ worth suffering for

From Irvine, being on my journey to Christ's Palace in Aberdeen
4 August 1636

Well-beloved and reverend Brother:

Grace, mercy and peace be to you. Upon acquaintance in Christ, I thought good to take the opportunity of writing to you. Seeing it hath seemed good to the Lord of the harvest to take the hooks out of our hands for a time, and to lay upon us a more honourable service, even to suffer for his name, it were good to comfort one another in writing. I have had a desire to see you in the face; yet now being the prisoner of Christ, it is taken away. I am greatly comforted to hear of your soldier's stately spirit for your princely and royal Captain Jesus our Lord, and for the grace of God in the rest of our dear brethren with you.

You have heard of my trouble, I suppose. It hath pleased our sweet Lord Jesus to let loose the malice of these interdicted lords in his house to deprive me of my ministry at Anwoth, and to confine me, eight score miles from thence, to Aberdeen; and also (which was not done to any before) to inhibit me to speak at all in Jesus' name within this kingdom, under the pain of rebellion. The cause that ripened their hatred was my book against the Arminians, whereof they accused me on those three days I appeared before them. But let our crowned King in Zion reign! By his grace the loss is theirs, the advantage is Christ's and truth's.

Albeit this honest cross gained some ground on me, and

my heaviness and my inward challenges of conscience for a
time were sharp, yet now, for the encouragement of you all,
I dare say it, and write it under my hand, 'Welcome, welcome,
sweet, sweet cross of Christ'. I verily think the chains of my
Lord Jesus are all overlaid with pure gold, and that his cross
is perfumed, and that it smelleth of Christ, and that the
victory shall be by the blood of the Lamb, and by the Word
of his truth, and that Christ, lying on his back in his weak
servants and oppressed truth, shall ride over his enemies'
bellies, and shall 'strike through kings in the day of his wrath'
[*Psalm* 110. 5]. It is time we laugh when he laugheth; and
seeing he is now pleased to sit with wrongs for a time, it
becometh us to be silent until the Lord hath let the enemies
enjoy their hungry, lean and feckless[1] paradise. Blessed are
they who are content to take strokes with weeping Christ.
Faith will trust the Lord, and is not hasty nor headstrong.
Neither is faith so timorous as to flatter a temptation or to
bud[2] and bribe the cross. It is little up or little down[3] that the
Lamb and his followers can get no law-surety, nor truce with
crosses; it must be so till we be up in our Father's house.

My heart is woe indeed for my mother Church that hath
played the harlot with many lovers. Her Husband hath a mind
to sell her for her horrible transgressions; and heavy will the
hand of the Lord be upon this backsliding nation. The ways
of our Zion mourn; her gold has become dim, her white
Nazarites are black like a coal. How shall not the children
weep when the Husband and the mother cannot agree! Yet
I believe Scotland's sky shall clear again; that Christ shall
build again the old waste places of Jacob; that our dry and
dead bones shall become one army of living men; and that
our Well-beloved may yet feed among the lilies, until the day
break and the shadows flee away [*Cant* 4. 5-6].

My dear brother, let us help one another with our prayers.
Our King shall mow down his enemies and shall come from

[1] Worthless.   [2] To win over by means of a gift.   [3] Of little moment.

Bozrah with his garments all dyed in blood. And for our consolation shall he appear, and call his wife Hephzibah and his land Beulah [*Is* 62. 4]; for he will rejoice over us and marry us, and Scotland shall say, 'What have I to do any more with idols?' Only let us be faithful to him that can ride through hell and death upon a windlestrae[1], and his horse never stumble. And let us make him a bridge over a water, so that his high and holy name may be glorified in me.

Strokes with the sweet Mediator's hand are very sweet. He was always sweet to my soul; but since I suffered for him, his breath hath a sweeter smell than before. O that every hair of my head, and every member and every bone in my body, were a man to witness a fair confession for him! I would think all too little for him. When I look over beyond the line, and beyond death, to the laughing side of the world, I triumph and ride upon the high places of Jacob; howbeit otherwise I am a faint, dead-hearted, cowardly man, oft borne down, and hungry in waiting for the marriage supper of the Lamb. Nevertheless I think it the Lord's wise love that feeds us with hunger, and makes us fat with wants and desertions.

I know not, my dear brother, if our worthy brethren be gone to sea or not.[2] They are on my heart and in my prayers. If they be yet with you, salute my dear friend, John Stuart, my well-beloved brethren in the Lord, Mr Blair, Mr Hamilton, Mr Livingston and Mr M'Clelland, and acquaint them with my troubles, and entreat them to pray for the poor afflicted prisoner of Christ. They are dear to my soul. I seek your prayers and theirs for my flock; their remembrance breaketh my heart. I desire to love that people, and others my dear acquaintance in Christ, with love in God and as God loveth them. I know that he who sent me to the west and south sends me also to the north. I will charge my soul to believe

---

[1] A withered stalk of grass; metaphorically a mere trifle.
[2] That is, to New England.

and to wait for him, and will follow his providence and not go before it nor stay behind it.

Now, my dear brother, taking farewell in paper, I commend you all to the Word of his grace, and to the work of his Spirit, to him who holdeth the seven stars in his right hand, that you may be kept spotless till the day of Jesus our Lord.

13/TO ALEXANDER GORDON, OF EARLSTON

His feelings upon leaving Anwoth

Edinburgh, 5 September 1636

Much honoured Sir:

I intend after the council-day to go on to Aberdeen: the Lord is with me, I care not what man can do. I burden no man, and I want nothing; no king is better provided than I am: sweet, sweet and easy is the cross of my Lord; all men I look in the face, of whatsoever rank, nobles and poor, acquaintance and strangers, are friendly to me. My Well-beloved is kinder and more warm than ordinary, and cometh and visiteth my soul: my chains are over-gilded with gold.

Only the remembrance of my fair days with Christ in Anwoth, and of my dear flock (whose case is my heart's sorrow) is vinegar to my sugared wine; yet both sweet and sour feed my soul. No pen, no words, no engine,[1] can express to you the loveliness of my only, only Lord Jesus. Thus in haste, I make for my palace at Aberdeen. I bless you, your wife, your eldest son and other children. Grace, grace be with you.

[1] Ability, disposition.

14/TO LADY KENMURE

Rutherford's enjoyment of Christ in Aberdeen
A sight of Christ exceeds all reports
Some are ashamed of Christ and His people

Aberdeen, 22 November 1636

My very Honourable and dear Lady:

Grace, mercy and peace be to you. I cannot forget your Ladyship and that sweet child. I desire to hear what the Lord is doing to you and him. To write to me were charity. I cannot but write to my friends, that Christ hath trysted me in Aberdeen; and my adversaries have sent me here to be feasted with love banquets with my royal, high, high, and princely Lord Jesus. Madam, why should I smother Christ's honesty? I dare not conceal his goodness to my soul. He looked fremed[1] and unco-like[2] upon me when I came first here; but I believe himself better than his looks. I shall not again quarrel Christ for a gloom[3] now he hath taken the mask off his face and saith, 'Kiss thy fill'. And what can I have more when I get great heaven in my little arms?

O how sweet are the sufferings of Christ for Christ! God forgive them that raise an ill report upon the sweet cross of Christ. It is but our weak and dim eyes, and our looking only to the black side, that makes us mistake. Those who can take that crabbed tree handsomely upon their back, and fasten it on cannily, shall find it such a burden as wings unto a bird or sails to a ship. Madam, rue not of your having chosen the better part. Upon my salvation, this is Christ's truth I now suffer for. If I found but cold comfort in my sufferings I would not beguile others; I would have told you plainly. But the

[1]Strange, distant.   [2]Uncommon, strange, uncouth.   [3]Frown.

truth is, Christ's crown, his sceptre, and the freedom of his kingdom is that which is now called in question; because we will not allow that Christ should pay tribute and be a vassal to the shields of the earth, therefore the sons of our mother are angry at us. But it becometh not Christ to hold any man's stirrup. It were a sweet and honourable death to die for the honour of that royal and princely King Jesus. His love is a mystery to the world. I would not have believed that there was so much in Christ as there is. 'Come and see' maketh Christ to be known in his excellency and glory. I wish all this nation knew how sweet his breath is. It is little to see Christ in a book, as men do the world in a card. They talk of Christ by the book and the tongue and no more; but to come nigh Christ and hause[1] him and embrace him is another thing.

Madam, I write for your honour, for your encouragement in that honourable profession Christ hath honoured you with. You have gotten the sunny side of the brae, and the best of Christ's good things. He hath not given you the bastard's portion. And howbeit you get strokes and sour looks from your Lord, yet believe his love more than your own feeling, for this world can take nothing from you that is truly yours, and death can do you no wrong. Your rock doth not ebb and flow, but your sea. That which Christ hath said, he will bide by it. He will be your tutor. You shall not get you charters of heaven to play you with. It is good that you have not lost your credit with Christ and that Lord Free-will shall not be your tutor. Christ will lippen[2] the taking you to heaven, neither to yourself nor any deputy, but only to himself. Blessed be your tutor! When your Head shall appear, your Bridegroom and Lord, your day shall then dawn, and it shall never have an afternoon nor an evening shadow. Let your child be Christ's; let him stay beside you as thy Lord's pledge that you shall willingly render again, if God will.

Madam, I find folks here kind to me, but in the night, and

[1]Clasp. [2]Entrust.

under their breath. My Master's cause may not come to the crown of the causeway. Others are kind according to their fashion. Many think me a strange man and my cause not good; but I care not much for man's thoughts or approbation. I think no shame of the cross. The preachers of the town pretend great love, but the prelates have added to the rest this gentle cruelty (for so they think of it) to discharge me of the pulpits of this town. The people murmur and cry out against it; and to speak truly (howbeit Christ is most indulgent to me otherwise), my silence on the Lord's day keeps me from being exalted above measure and from startling[1] in the heat of my Lord's love. Some people affect[2] me, for the which cause I hear the preachers here purpose to have my confinement changed to another place; so cold is northern love; but Christ and I will bear it. I have wrestled long with this sad silence. I said, what aileth Christ at my service? and my soul hath been at a pleading with Christ, and at yea and nay. But I will yield to him, providing my suffering may preach more than my tongue did; for I give not Christ an inch but for twice as good again. In a word, I am a fool, and he is God. I will hold my peace hereafter.

Let me hear from your Ladyship and your dear child. Pray for the prisoner of Christ who is mindful of your Ladyship. Remember my obliged obedience to my good Lady Marr. Grace, grace be with you. I write and pray blessings to your sweet child.

[1] Acting strangely or excitedly (as cattle do in hot weather).
[2] Show affection to.

15/TO HUGH M'KAIL

Christ to be trusted amid trial

Aberdeen, 22 November 1636

Reverend and dear Brother:

I thank you for your letter. I cannot but show you, that as I never expected anything from Christ but much good and kindness, so he hath made me to find it in the house of my pilgrimage. And believe me, brother, I give it to you under mine own hand-writ, that whoso looketh to the white side of Christ's cross, and can take it up handsomely with faith and courage, shall find it such a burden as sails are to a ship or wings to a bird. I find that my Lord hath overgilded that black tree, and hath perfumed it, and oiled it with joy and consolation. Like a fool, once I would chide and plead with Christ, and slander him to others, of unkindness. But I trust in God not to call his glooms unkind again; for he hath taken from me my sackcloth; and I verily cannot tell you what a poor Joseph and prisoner (with whom my mother's children were angry) doth now think of kind Christ.

I will chide no more, providing he will quit me all by-gones; for I am poor. I am taught in this ill weather to go on the lee-side of Christ, and to put him in between me and the storm; and (I thank God) I walk on the sunny side of the brae. I write it that ye may speak in my behalf the praises of my Lord to others, that my bonds may preach. O, if all Scotland knew the feasts and love-blinks and visits that the prelates have sent unto me, I will verily give my Lord Jesus a free discharge of all that I, like a fool, laid to his charge, and beg him pardon, to the mends. God grant that in my temptations I come not on his wrong side again, and never again fall araving against my Physician in my fever.

Brother, plead with your mother while ye have time. A pulpit would be a high feast to me, but I dare not say one word against him who hath done it. I am not out of the house as yet. My sweet Master saith I shall have houseroom at his own elbow; albeit their synagogue will need force to cast me out. A letter were a work of charity to me. Grace be with you. Pray for me.

Your brother and Christ's prisoner,

S.R.

16/TO MARION M'NAUGHT

Comfort under tribulations
The prison a palace

Aberdeen, 3 January 1637

My dearly beloved Sister:

Grace, mercy and peace be to you. I complain that Galloway is not kind to me in paper. I have received no letters these sixteen weeks, but two. I am well. My prison is a palace to me, and Christ's banqueting-house. My Lord Jesus is as kind as they call him. O that all Scotland knew my case and had part of my feast! I charge you in the name of God, I charge you to believe. Fear not the sons of men; the worms shall eat them. To pray and believe now, when Christ seems to give you a nay-say, is more than it was before. Die believing; die, and Christ's promise in your hand! I desire, I request, I charge your husband and that town,[1] to stand for the truth of the Gospel. Contend with Christ's enemies; and I pray

[1] Kirkcudbright.

you show all professors whom you know my case. Help me to praise. The ministers here envy me; they will have my prison changed. My mother hath borne me a man of contention, and one that striveth with the whole earth. Remember my love to your husband. Grace be with you.

17/TO JOHN GORDON OF CARDONESS, ELDER

Win Christ at all hazards
Christ's beauty
A word to children

Aberdeen 1637

Much honoured Sir:

Grace, mercy and peace be to you. I have longed to hear from you and to know the estate of your soul, and the estate of that people with you. I beseech you, Sir, by the salvation of your precious soul and the mercies of God, to make good and sure work of your salvation, and try upon what groundstone you have builded. Worthy and dear Sir, if you be upon sinking sand, a storm of death and a blast will lose Christ and you, and wash you close off the rock. O for the Lord's sake look narrowly to the work!

Read over your life, with the light of God's day-light and sun; for salvation is not casten down at every man's door. It is good to look to your compass, and all ye have need of, ere you take shipping; for no wind can blow you back again. Remember, when the race is ended, and the play either won or lost, and ye are in the utmost circle and border of time, and shall put your foot within the march[1] of eternity, and

[1]Boundary, border.

all your good things of this short night-dream shall seem to you like the ashes of a bleeze[1] of thorns or straw, and your poor soul shall be crying, 'Lodging, lodging, for God's sake!', then shall your soul be more glad at one of your Lord's lovely and homely smiles than if you had the charters of three worlds for all eternity. Let pleasures and gain, will and desires of this world, be put over into God's hands, as arrested and fenced goods that ye cannot intromit[2] with. Now, when ye are drinking the grounds[3] of your cup, and ye are upon the utmost end of the last link of time, and old age like death's long shadow is casting a covering upon your days, it is no time to court this vain life, and to set love and heart upon it. It is near after-supper; seek rest and ease for your soul in God through Christ.

Believe me, that I find it to be hard wrestling to play fair with Christ, and to keep good quarters with him, and to love him in integrity and life, and to keep a constant course of sound and solid daily communion with Christ. Temptations are daily breaking the thread of that course, and it is not easy to cast a knot again; and many knots make evil work. O how fair have many ships been plying before the wind, that, in an hour's space, have been lying in the sea-bottom! How many professors cast a golden lustre, as if they were pure gold, and yet are, under that skin and cover, but base and reprobate metal! And how many keep breath in their race many miles, and yet come short of the prize and the garland! Dear Sir, my soul would mourn in secret for you, if I knew your case with God to be but false work. Love to have you anchored upon Christ maketh me fear your tottering and slips. False underwater, not seen in the ground of an enlightened conscience, is dangerous; so is often falling and sinning against light. Know this, that those who never had sick nights or days in conscience for sin, cannot have but

---

[1]A sudden flaming up.   [2]Intermeddle with, handle.   [3]Dregs.

such a peace with God as will uncercoat[1] and break the flesh again, and end in a sad war at death. O how fearfully are thousands beguiled with false hide, grown over old sins, as if the soul were cured and healed!

Dear Sir, I always saw nature mighty, lofty, heady and strong in you; and that it was more for you to be mortified and dead to the world than for another common man. You will take a low ebb, and a deep cut, and a long lance, to go to the bottom of your wounds in saving humiliation, to make you a won prey for Christ. Be humbled; walk softly. Down, down, for God's sake, my dear and worthy brother, with your topsail. Stoop, stoop! it is a low entry to go in at heaven's gate. There is infinite justice in the party you have to deal with; it is his nature not to acquit the guilty and the sinner. The law of God will not want one farthing of the sinner. God forgetteth not both the cautioner and the sinner; and every man must pay, either in his own person (O, Lord save you from this payment!) or in his cautioner[2], Christ.

It is violence to corrupt nature for a man to be holy, to lie down under Christ's feet, to quit will, pleasure, worldly love, earthly hope, and an itching of heart after this farded[3] and over-gilded world, and to be content that Christ trample upon all. Come in, come in to Christ, and see what ye want, and find it in him. He is the short cut (as we used to say) and the nearest way to an outgate[4] of all your burdens. I dare avouch that ye shall be dearly welcome to him. My soul would be glad to take part of the joy ye should have in him. I dare say that angels' pens, angels' tongues, nay, as many worlds of angels as there are drops of water in all the seas and fountains and rivers of the earth, cannot paint him out to you. I think his sweetness since I was a prisoner hath swelled upon me to the greatness of two heavens. O for a soul as wide as the utmost circle of the highest heaven that containeth

[1]Fester under the skin. [2]Surety, security.
[3]Painted, coloured. [4]Way of escape.

all, to contain his love!

And yet I could hold little of it. O world's wonder! Oh, if my soul might but lie within the smell of his love, suppose I could get no more but the smell of it! Oh, but it is long to that day when I shall have a free world of Christ's love! O what a sight to be up in heaven, in that fair orchard of the new paradise, and to see and smell and touch and kiss that fair field-flower, that ever-green Tree of Life! His bare shadow were enough for me. A sight of him would be the earnest of heaven to me. Fy, fy upon us! that we have love lying rusting beside us or, which is worse, wasting upon some loathsome objects, and that Christ should lie his lone. Woe, woe is me! that sin hath made so many madmen, seeking the fool's paradise, fire under ice, and some good and desirable things, without and apart from Christ. Christ, Christ, nothing but Christ can cool our love's burning languor. O thirsty love! wilt thou set Christ, the well of life, to thy head, and drink thy fill? Drink and spare not; drink love and be drunken with Christ! Nay, alas! the distance betwixt us and Christ is a death. O, if we were clasped in other's arms! We should never twin[1] again, except heaven twinned and sundered us; and that cannot be.

I desire your children to seek the Lord. Desire them from me, to be requested for Christ's sake to be blessed and happy, and to come and take Christ and all things with him. Let them beware of glassy and slippery youth, of foolish young notions, of worldly lusts, of deceivable gain, of wicked company, of cursing, lying, blaspheming and foolish talking. Let them be filled with the Spirit, acquaint themselves with daily praying, and with the storehouse of wisdom and comfort, the good Word of God. Help the souls of the poor people. O that my Lord would bring me again among you, that I might tell unco[2] and great tales of Christ to them! Receive not a stranger to preach any other doctrine to them.

[1]Separate. [2]See *p43 fn* 2.

Pray for me, his prisoner of hope. I pray for you without ceasing. I write my blessing, earnest prayers, the love of God, and the sweet presence of Christ to you and yours and them. Grace, grace, grace be with you.

Your lawful and loving pastor,

S.R.

18/TO ROBERT BLAIR

God's arrangements sometimes mysterious

Aberdeen, 7 February 1637

Reverend and dearly beloved Brother:

Grace, mercy and peace from God our Father and from our Lord Jesus Christ, be unto you.

It is no great wonder, my dear brother, that you be in heaviness for a season, and that God's will (in crossing your design and desires to dwell amongst a people whose God is the Lord) should move you. I deny not but you have cause to inquire what his providence speaketh in this to you; but God's directing and commanding will can by no good logic be concluded from events of providence. The Lord sent Paul on many errands for the spreading of his Gospel, where he found lions in his way. A promise was made to his people of the Holy Land, and yet many nations were in the way, fighting against and ready to kill them that had the promise, or to keep them from possessing that good land which the Lord their God had given them.

I know that you have most to do with submission of spirit; but I persuade myself that you have learned, in every condition wherein you are cast, therein to be content and to say, 'Good is the will of the Lord, let it be done'. I believe that the Lord tacketh his ship often to fetch the wind, and that he purposeth to bring mercy out of your sufferings and silence which (I know from mine own experience) is grievous to you. Seeing that he knoweth our willing mind to serve him, our wages and stipend is running to the fore with our God, even as some sick soldiers get pay when they are bedfast and not able to go to the field with others. 'Though Israel be not gathered, yet shall I be glorious in the eyes of the Lord, and my God shall be my strength' [*Is* 49. 5]. And we are to believe it shall be thus ere all the play be played. 'The violence done to me and to my flesh be upon Babylon' (and the great whore's lovers) 'shall the inhabitant of Zion say; and my blood be upon Chaldea, shall Jerusalem say' [*Jer* 51. 35].

'And behold, I will make Jerusalem a cup of trembling to all the people round about, when they shall be in the siege both against Judah and against Jerusalem. And in that day will I make Jerusalem a burdensome stone for all people: they that burden themselves with it shall be broken in pieces, though all the people of the earth be gathered together against it' [*Zech* 12. 2-3].When they have eaten and swallowed us up, they shall be sick and vomit us out living men again; the devil's stomach cannot digest the Church of God. Suffering is the other half of our ministry, howbeit the hardest; for we would be content that our King Jesus should make an open proclamation, and cry down crosses, and cry up joy, gladness, ease, honour and peace. But it must not be so. Through many afflictions we must enter into the kingdom of God. Not only by them, but through them, must we go, and wiles will not take us past the cross. It is folly to think to steal to heaven with a whole skin.

For myself, I am here a prisoner confined in Aberdeen, threatened to be removed to Caithness because I desire to edify in this town; and am openly preached against in the pulpits in my hearing, and tempted with disputations by the doctors, especially by D.B.[1] Yet I am not ashamed of the Lord

[1] Dr Robert Barron, Professor of Divinity in the Marischal College of Aberdeen.

Jesus, his garland and his crown. I would not exchange my weeping with the painted laughter of the fourteen prelates. At my first coming here I took the dorts[1] at Christ and would, forsooth, summon him for unkindness. I sought a plea of my Lord and was tossed with challenges whether he loved me or not, and disputed over again all that he had done to me, because his word was a fire shut up in my bowels, and I was weary with forbearing, because I said I was cast out of the Lord's inheritance. But now I see that I was a fool. My Lord miskent[2] all and did bear with my foolish jealousies, and miskent that ever I wronged his love.

And now he has come again with mercy under his wings. I pass from my (O witless!) summons. He is God, I see, and I am man. Now it hath pleased him to renew his love to my soul and to dawt[3] his poor prisoner. Therefore, dear brother, help me to praise and show the Lord's people with you what he hath done to my soul, that they may pray and praise. And I charge you, in the name of Christ, not to omit it. For this cause I write to you, that my sufferings may glorify my royal King and edify his Church in Ireland. He knoweth how one of Christ's live coals hath burnt my soul with a desire to have my bonds to preach his glory, whose cross I now bear. God forgive you if you do it not. But I hope the Lord will move your heart to proclaim in my behalf the sweetness, excellency and glory of my royal King. It is but our soft flesh that hath raised a slander on the Cross of Christ: I see now the white side of it; my Lord's chains are all over-gilded. O if Scotland and Ireland had part of my feast! And yet I get not my meat but with many strokes. There are none here to whom I can speak; I dwell in Kedar's tents. Refresh me with a letter from you. Few know what is betwixt Christ and me.

Dear brother, upon my salvation, this is his truth that we suffer for. Christ would not seal a blank charter to souls.

[1]Sulks. [2]Overlooked.
[3] Pet, show favour to.

Courage, courage! joy, joy for evermore! O joy unspeakable and glorious! O for help to set my crowned King on high! O for love to him who is altogether lovely!—that love which many waters cannot quench, neither can the floods drown!

I remember you and bear your name on my breast to Christ. I beseech you, forget not his afflicted prisoner. Grace, mercy and peace be with you.

19/TO ROBERT GORDON OF KNOCKBRECK

Visits of Christ
Things which affliction teaches

Aberdeen, 9 February 1637

My very worthy and dear Friend:

Grace, mercy and peace be to you. Though all Galloway should have forgotten me, I would have expected a letter from you ere now; but I will not expound it to be forgetfulness of me.

Now, my dear brother, I cannot show you how matters go betwixt Christ and me. I find my Lord going and coming seven times a day. His visits are short, but they are both frequent and sweet. I dare not for my life think of a challenge of my Lord. I hear ill tales and hard reports of Christ from the tempter and my flesh; but love believeth no evil. I may swear that they are liars, and the apprehensions make lies of Christ's honest and unalterable love to me. I dare not say that I am a dry tree or that I have no room at all in the vineyard; but yet I often think that the sparrows are blessed, who may resort to the house of God in Anwoth, from which I am banished.

Temptations that I supposed to be stricken dead and laid upon their back rise again and revive upon me; yea, I see that, while I live, temptations will not die. The devil seemeth to brag and boast as much as if he had more court with Christ than I have, and as if he had charmed and blasted my ministry, that I shall do no more good in public. But his wind shaketh no corn.[1] I will not believe that Christ would have made such a mint[2] to have me to himself, and have taken so much pains upon me as he hath done, and then slip so easily from possession, and lose the glory of what he hath done. Nay, since I came to Aberdeen, I have been taken up to see the new land, the fair palace of the Lamb; and will Christ let me see heaven, to break my heart and never give it to me? I shall not think my Lord Jesus giveth a dumb earnest, or putteth his seals to blank paper, or intendeth to put me off with fair and false promises.

I see that now which I never saw well before:

1. I see faith's necessity in a fair day is never known aright; but now I miss nothing so much as faith. Hunger in me runneth to fair and sweet promises; but when I come, I am like a hungry man that wanteth teeth, or a weak stomach having a sharp appetite that is filled with the very sight of meat, or like one stupified with cold under the water, that would fain come to land but cannot grip anything casten to him. I can let Christ grip me, but I cannot grip him. I love to be kissed, and to sit on Christ's knee; but I cannot set my feet to the ground, for afflictions bring the cramp upon my faith. All that I can do is to hold out a lame faith to Christ like a beggar holding out a stump, instead of an arm or leg, and cry, 'Lord Jesus, work a miracle!' O what would I give to have hands and arms to grip strongly and fold handsomely about Christ's neck, and to have my claim made good with real possession! I think that my love to Christ hath feet in abundance, and runneth swiftly to be at him, but it wanteth hands and fingers to apprehend him. I think that I would give Christ every morning my

---

[1] Does no harm.   [2] Attempt.

blessing, to have as much faith as I have love and hunger; at least I miss faith more than love or hunger.

2. I see that mortification, and to be crucified to the world, is not so highly accounted of by us as it should be. O how heavenly a thing it is to be dead and dumb and deaf to this world's sweet music! I confess it hath pleased His Majesty to make me laugh at the children who are wooing this world for their match. I see men lying about the world, as nobles about a king's court, and I wonder what they are all doing there. As I am at this present I would scorn to court such a feckless[1] and petty princess, or buy this world's kindness with a bow of my knee. I scarce now either see or hear what it is that this world offereth me; I know that it is little which it can take from me and as little that it can give me. I recommend mortification to you above anything; for, alas! we but chase feathers flying in the air, and tire our own spirits for the froth and over-gilded clay of a dying life. One sight of what my Lord hath let me see within this short time is worth a world of worlds.

3. I thought courage, in the time of trouble for Christ's sake, a thing that I might take up at my foot. I thought that the very remembrance of the honesty of the cause would be enough. But I was a fool in so thinking. I have much ado now to win to one smile. But I see that joy groweth up in heaven, and it is above our short arm. Christ will be steward and dispenser himself, and none else but he. Therefore, now, I count much of one dramweight of spiritual joy. One smile of Christ's face is now to me as a kingdom; and yet He is no niggard to me of comforts. Truly I have no cause to say that I am pinched with penury or that the consolations of Christ are dried up; for he hath poured down rivers upon a dry wilderness the like of me, to my admiration; and in my very swoonings he holdeth up my head and stayeth me with flagons of wine, and

[1] See *p* 40 *fn* 1.

comforteth me with apples. My house and bed are strewed with kisses of love. Praise, praise with me. O if you and I betwixt us could lift up Christ upon his throne, howbeit all Scotland should cast him down to the ground!

My brother's case toucheth me near. I hope that you will be kind to him and give him your best counsel.

Remember my love to your brother, to your wife, and G.M. Desire him to be faithful and to repent of his hypocrisy; and say that I wrote it to you. I wish him salvation. Write to me your mind anent C.E. and C.Y, and their wives, and I.G. or any others in my parish.[1] I fear that I am forgotten amongst them, but I cannot forget them.

The prisoner's prayers and blessings come upon you. Grace, grace be with you.

20/TO LADY KENMURE

None worthy but Christ
'Anwoth is not heaven'

Aberdeen 1637

Madam:

Notwithstanding the great haste of the bearer, I would bless your Ladyship on paper, desiring, that since Christ hath ever envied that the world should have your love by him,[2] that you give yourself out for Christ, and that you may be for no other. I know none worthy of you but Christ. Madam, I am either suffering for Christ, and this is either the sure and good way, or I have done with heaven, and shall never see God's face, which, I bless him, cannot be.

I write my blessing to that sweet child, whom you have

---

[1] The initials are those of various parishioners in Anwoth.
[2] That is, more than he (setting him aside)

borrowed from God; he is no heritage to you, but a loan; love him as folks do borrowed things; my heart is heavy for you. They say the kirk of Christ hath neither son nor heir; and therefore her enemies shall possess her; but I know she is not so ill-friended, her Husband is her heir, and she his heritage.

If my Lord would be pleased, I would desire some were dealt with for my return to Anwoth; but if that never be, thank God, Anwoth is not heaven, preaching is not Christ; I hope to wait on. Let me hear how the child is, and your Ladyship's mind and hopes of him; for it would ease my heart to know that he is well. I am in good terms with Christ; but oh, my guiltiness! yet he bringeth not pleas betwixt him and me to the streets, and before the sun. Grace, grace, for evermore, be with your Ladyship.

21/TO DAVID DICKSON

God's dealings
The bitter sweetened
Notes on Scripture

Aberdeen, 7 March 1637

Reverend and dearest Brother:

What joy have I out of heaven's gates but that my Lord Jesus be glorified in my bonds? Blessed be thou of the Lord who contribute anything to my obliged and indebted praises. Dear brother, help me, a poor dyvour,[1] to pay the interest; for I cannot come nigh to render the principal. It is not jest or sport which maketh me to speak and write as I do: I never before came to that nick or pitch of communion with Christ that I have now attained to. For my confirmation, I have been these two Sabbaths or three in private, taking instruments[2] in

[1]Debtor (sometimes a bankrupt).   [2]Documents, furnishing proof.

the name of God, that my Lord Jesus and I have kissed each other in Aberdeen, the house of my pilgrimage. I seek not an apple to play me with (He knoweth, whom I serve in the spirit!), but a seal. I but beg earnest, and am content to suspend and frist[1] glory till suppertime.

I know that this world will not last with me; for my moon-light is noonday light, and my four hours[2] above my feasts when I was a preacher; at which time also I was embraced very often in his arms. But who can blame Christ to take me on behind him (if I may say so) on his white horse, or in his chariot, paved with love, through a water? Will not a father take his little dawted[3] Davie in his arms, and carry him over a ditch or a mire? My short legs could not step over this lair,[4] or sinking mire; and therefore, my Lord Jesus will bear me through. If a change come, and a dark day (so being that He will keep my faith without flaw or crack) I dare not blame him, howbeit I get no more till I come to heaven.

But you know that the physic behoved to have sugar: my faith was fallen aswoon, and Christ but held up a swooning man's head. Indeed, I pray not for a dawted child's diet, He knoweth that I would have Christ, sour or sweet – any way, so being it be Christ indeed. I stand not now upon pared apples, or sugared dishes, but I cannot blame him to give, and I must gape and make a wide mouth. Since Christ will not pantry up[5] joys, he must be welcome who will not bide away. I seek no other fruit that he may be glorified. He knoweth that I would take hard fare to have his name set on high.

I bless you for your counsel. I hope to live by faith and swim without a mass or bundle of joyful sense under my chin; at least to venture, albeit I should be ducked.

Now for my case: I think that the Council should be essayed, and the event referred to God – duties are ours and events are God's.

[1]To postpone possession. [2]Afternoon meal (taken four hours after morning meal). [3]See *p54 fn 4*. [4]Bog. [5]Lock up in the cupboard.

I shall go through yours upon the Covenant at leisure, and write to you my mind thereanent: and anent the Arminian contract betwixt the Father and the Son. I beseech you, set to, to go through Scripture. Yours on the Hebrews is in great request with all who would be acquainted with Christ's Testament. I purpose, God willing, to set about Hosea and to try if I can get it to the press here.[1]

It refresheth me much that you are so kind to my brother. I hope your counsel will do him good. I recommend him to you, since I am so far from him. I am glad that the dying servant of God, famous and faithful Mr Cunningham, sealed your ministry before he fell asleep.

Grace, grace be with you.

22/TO ALEXANDER HENDERSON

Sadness because Christ's Headship not set forth
Christ's cause attended with crosses
The believer seen of all

Aberdeen, 9 March 1637

My Reverend and dear Brother:

I received your letters. They are as apples of gold to me; for with my sweet feasts (and they are above the deserving of such a sinner, high and out of measure), I have sadness to ballast me and weigh me a little. It is but his boundless wisdom which hath taken the tutoring of his witless child. And he knoweth

[1] Ministers of the Word had planned to produce short commentaries on the entire Bible. Dickson wrote on The Psalms, Matthew and Hebrews. Rutherford did not fulfil his desire to write on Hosea; the work was later accomplished by George Hutcheson.

that to be drunken with comforts is not safest for our stomachs. However it be, the din and noise and glooms[1] of Christ's cross are weightier than itself. I protest to you (my witness is in heaven) that I could wish many pound weights added to my cross, to know that by my sufferings Christ were set forward in his kingly office in this land. O what is my skin to his glory! or my losses, or my sad heart, to the apple of the eye of our Lord and his beloved Spouse, his precious truth, his royal privileges, the glory of manifested justice in giving his foes a dash, the testimony of his faithful servants who do glorify him, when he rideth upon poor weak worms, and triumpheth in them! I desire you to pray that I may come out of this furnace with honesty, and that I may leave Christ's truth no worse than I found it; and that this most honourable cause may neither be stained nor weakened.

As for your cause, my reverend and dearest brother, you are the talk of the north and south, and looked to, so as if you were all crystal glass. Your motes and dust would soon be proclaimed and trumpets blown at your slips. But I know that ye have laid help upon One that is mighty. Entrust not your comforts to men's airy and frothy applause, neither lay your down-castings on the tongues of salt[2] mockers and reproachers of godliness. 'As deceivers, and yet true; as unknown, and yet well-known' [2 *Cor* 6. 8-9]. God hath called you to Christ's side, and the wind is now in Christ's face in this land. And seeing you are with him you cannot expect the lee-side or the sunny side of the brae. But I know that you have resolved to take Christ upon any terms whatsoever. I hope that you do not rue, though your cause be hated, and prejudices are taken up against it. The shields of the world think our Master cumbersome wares, and that he maketh too great din, and that his cords and yokes make blains and deep scores in their neck. Therefore they kick. They say, 'This man shall not reign over us'.

[1] See *p* 43 *fn* 3   [2] Sarcastic.

Let us pray one for another. He who hath made you a chosen arrow in his quiver, hide you in the hollow of his hand!

23/TO JOHN GORDON, YOUNGER

Reasons for being earnest about the soul
Resignation

Aberdeen [undated]

Honoured and dear Brother:

I wrote of late to you: multitudes of letters burden me now. I am refreshed with your letter.

I exhort you in the bowels of Christ, set to work for your soul. And let these bear weight with you, and ponder them seriously.

1. Weeping and gnashing of teeth in utter darkness, or heaven's joy.
2. Think what you would give for an hour, when you shall lie like dead, cold, blackened clay.
3. There is sand in your glass yet, and your sun is not gone down.
4. Consider what joy and peace are in Christ's service.
5. Think what advantage it will be to have angels, the world, life and death, crosses, yea, and devils, all for you, as the King's serjeants and servants, to do your business.
6. To have mercy on your seed and a blessing on your house.
7. To have true honour and a name on earth that casteth a sweet smell.
8. How ye will rejoice when Christ layeth down your head under his chin, and betwixt his breasts, and drieth your

face, and welcometh you to glory and happiness.

9. Imagine what pain and torture is a guilty conscience; what slavery to carry the devil's dishonest loads.

10. Sin's joys are but night-dreams, thoughts, vapours, imaginations, and shadows.

11. What dignity it is to be a son of God.

12. Dominion and mastery over temptations, over the world and sin.

13. That your enemies should be the tail and you the head.

For your children now at rest (I speak to you and your wife, and cause her read this):

1. I am a witness for Barbara's glory in heaven.

2. For the rest, I write it under my hand, there are days coming on Scotland when barren wombs and dry breasts and childless parents shall be pronounced blessed. They are, then, in the lee of the harbour ere the storm come on.

3. They are not lost to you that are laid up in Christ's treasury in heaven.

4. At the resurrection you shall meet with them; thither they are sent before but not sent away.

5. Your Lord loveth you, who is homely to take and give, borrow and lend.

6. Let not children be your idols, for God will be jealous and take away the idol, because he is greedy of your love wholly.

I bless you, your wife and children. Grace for evermore be with you.

Your loving pastor,

S.R.

24/TO MARION M'NAUGHT

Adherence to duty amidst opposition
The power of Christ's love

Aberdeen, 9 March 1637

Loving and dear Sister:

Grace, mercy and peace be to you. Your letter hath refreshed my soul. You shall not have my advice to make haste to go out of that town, for if you remove out of Kirkcudbright, they will easily undo all. You are at God's work, and in his way there. Be strong in the Lord; the devil is weaker than you are, because stronger is he that is in you than he that is in the world. Your care of and love showed towards me, now a prisoner of Christ, is laid up for you in heaven, and you shall know that it is come up in remembrance before God.

Pray, pray for my desolate flock, and give them your counsel when you meet with any of them. It shall be my grief to hear that a wolf enters in upon my labours; but if the Lord permit it, I am silent. My sky shall clear, for Christ layeth my head in his bosom and admitteth me to lean there. I never knew before what his love was in such a measure. If he leave me, he leaveth me in pain, and sick of love. And yet my sickness is my life and health. I have a fire within me; I defy all the devils in hell, and all the prelates in Scotland, to cast water on it.

I rejoice at your courage and faith. Pray still, as if I were on my journey to come and be your pastor. What iron gates or bars are able to stand it out against Christ? for when he bloweth, they open to him.

I remember your husband. Grace, grace be with you.

25/TO WILLIAM LIVINGSTONE
   Counsel to a youth

Aberdeen, 13 March 1637

My very dear brother:

I rejoice to hear that Christ hath run away with your young love, and that you are, so early in the morning, matched with such a Lord; for a young man is often a dressed lodging for the devil to dwell in. Be humble and thankful for grace, and judge it not so much by weight, as by its truth. Christ will not cast water on your smoking coal, he never yet put out a dim candle that was lighted at the Sun of Righteousness.

I recommend to you prayer and watching over the sins of your youth; for I know that missive letters go between the devil and young blood. Satan hath a friend at court in the heart of youth; and there pride, luxury, lust, revenge, forgetfulness of God, are hired as his agents. Happy is your soul if Christ man the house, and take the keys himself, and command all (as it suiteth him full well to rule all wherever he is). Keep and entertain Christ well; cherish his grace; blow upon your own coal, and let him tutor you.

Now, for myself, know that I am fully agreed with my Lord. Christ hath put the Father and me in each other's arms. Many a sweet bargain he made before, and he hath made this among the rest. I reign, as king, over my crosses; I will not flatter a temptation, nor give the devil a good word; I defy hell's iron gates. God hath passed over my quarrelling against him at my entry here, and now he feedeth and feasteth with me. Praise, praise with me, and let us exalt his name together.

26/TO THE LAIRD OF CARLETON

Increasing sense of Christ's love
Resignation
Deadness to earth
Temptations and infirmities

Aberdeen, 14 March 1637

Much honoured Sir:

I will not impute your not writing to me to forgetfulness; however, I have One above who forgetteth me not; nay, he groweth in his kindness. It hath pleased His holy Majesty to take me from the pulpit, and teach me many things in my exile and prison that were mysteries to me before; as,

1. I see his bottomless and boundless love and kindness, and my jealousies and ravings, which, at my first entry into this furnace, were so foolish and bold as to say to Christ, who is Truth itself, in his face, 'Thou liest'. I had well nigh lost my grips; I wondered if it was Christ or not; for the mist and smoke of my perturbed heart made me mistake my Master, Jesus. My faith was dim, and hope frozen and cold; and my love, which caused jealousies, had some warmness, and heat, and smoke, but no flame at all. Yet I was looking for some good of Christ's old claim to me, though I had forfeited all my rights. But the tempter was too much upon my counsels, and was still blowing the coal. Alas! I knew not well before what good skill my Intercessor and Advocate, Christ, hath in pleading, and in pardoning me such follies. Now he is returned to my soul 'with healing in his wings'; and I am nothing behind with

Christ now, for he hath overpaid me, by his presence, the pain I was put to by on-waiting, and any little loss I sustained by my witnessing against the wrongs done to him.

I think it was a pain to my Lord to hide himself any longer. In a manner, he was challenging his own unkindness, and repented him of his glooms.[1] And now, what want I on earth that Christ can give to a poor prisoner? O how sweet and lovely is he now! Alas! that I can get none to help me to lift up my Lord Jesus upon his throne, above all the earth!

2. I am now brought to some measure of submission, and I resolve to wait till I see what my Lord Jesus will do with me. I dare not now nickname, or speak one word against, the all-seeing and over-watching Providence of my Lord. I see Providence runneth not on broken wheels; but I, like a fool, carved a Providence for mine own ease, to die in my nest, and to sleep still, till my grey hairs, and to lie on the sunny side of the mountain, in my ministry at Anwoth. But now I have nothing to say against a borrowed fireside, and another man's house, nor Kedar's tents, where I live, being removed far from my acquaintance, my lovers and my friends. I see God hath the world on his wheels, and casteth it as a potter doth a vessel on the wheel. I dare not say that there is any inordinate or irregular motion in Providence. The Lord hath done it. I will not go to law with Christ, for I should gain nothing of that.

3. I have learned some greater mortification, and not to mourn after or seek to suck the world's dry breasts. Nay, my Lord hath filled me with such dainties that I am like a full banqueter, who is not for common cheer. What have I to do to fall down upon my knees, and worship mankind's great idol, the world? I have a better God than any clay-god. Nay, at present, as I am now disposed, I care not

[1] See p 43 *fn* 3.

much to give this world a discharge of my life – rent of it, for bread and water. I know it is not my home, nor my Father's house; it is but his footstool, his muir-ground.[1] Let bastards take it; I hope never to think myself in its common for honour or riches. Nay now I say to laughter, 'Thou art madness'.

4. I find it most true, that the greatest temptation out of hell is to live without temptations. If my waters would stand, they would rot. Faith is the better for the free air and the sharp winter-storm in its face. Grace withereth without adversity. The devil is but God's master-fencer, to teach us to handle our weapons.

5. I never knew how weak I was till now, when he hideth himself, and when I have him to seek seven times a day. I am a dry and withered branch, and a piece of a dead carcase, dry bones, and not able to step over a straw. The thoughts of my old sins are as the summons of death to me; and of late my brother's case hath stricken me to the heart. When my wounds are closing, a little ruffle causeth them to bleed afresh. So thin-skinned is my soul that I think it is like a tender man's skin, that may touch nothing; you see how short I should shoot of the prize if his grace were not sufficient for me.

Woe is me for the day of Scotland! Woe, woe is me for my harlot-mother; for the decree is gone forth! Women of this land shall call the childless and miscarrying wombs blessed. The anger of the Lord is gone forth, and shall not return, till he perform the purpose of his heart against Scotland. Yet he shall make Scotland a new sharp instrument having teeth to thresh the mountains, and fan the hills as chaff. The prisoner's blessing be upon you.

[1]Waste, heath-land.

27/TO JOHN FLEMING, BAILIE OF LEITH

Directions for Christian conduct

Aberdeen, 15 March 1637

Worthy and dearly beloved in the Lord:

Grace, mercy and peace be unto you. I received your letter: I wish I could satisfy your desires, in drawing up and framing for you a Christian Directory. But the learned have done it before me, more judiciously than I can; especially Mr Rogers,[1] Greenham,[2] and Perkins.[3] Notwithstanding, I will show you what I would have been at myself, although I came always short of my purpose.

1. That hours of the day, less or more time, for the Word and prayer, be given to God, not sparing the twelfth hour or mid-day, although it should then be a shorter time.
2. In the midst of worldly employments there should be some thoughts of sin, judgment, death and eternity, with a word or two (at least) of ejaculatory prayer to God.
3. To beware of wandering of heart in private prayers.
4. Not to grudge, although you come from prayer without sense of joy. Downcasting, sense of guiltiness, and hunger are often best for us.
5. That the Lord's day, from morning to night, be spent always either in private or public worship.
6. That words be observed, wandering and idle thoughts be avoided, sudden anger and desire of revenge, even of such

---

[1] Daniel Rogers (1573-1652) of Haversham (Bucks) and Wethersfield (Essex): he suffered under the Laudian persecution of the Puritans.
[2] Richard Greenham (1535-94?) of Cambridgeshire and London: an early Puritan.
[3] William Perkins (1558-1602) of Cambridge: eminent among the Elizabethan Puritans.

as persecute the truth, be guarded against; for we often mix our zeal with our own wild-fire.

7. That known, discovered and revealed sins, that are against the conscience, be avoided, as most dangerous preparatives to hardness of heart.

8. That in dealing with men, faith and truth in covenants and trafficking be regarded; that we deal with all men in sincerity; that conscience be made of idle and lying words; and that our carriage be such as that they who see it may speak honourably of our sweet Master and profession.

I have been much challenged,

1. For not referring all to God, as the last end: that I do not eat, drink, sleep, journey, speak and think for God.

2. That I have not benefited by good company; and that I left not some word of conviction, even upon natural and wicked men, as by reproving swearing in them; or because of being a silent witness to their loose carriage; and because I intended not in all companies to do good.

3. That the woes and calamities of the kirk, and particular professors, have not moved me.

4. That in reading the life of David, Paul, and the like, when it humbled me, I, coming so far short of their holiness, laboured not to imitate them, afar off at least, according to the measure of God's grace.

5. That unrepented sins of youth were not looked to and lamented for.

6. That sudden stirrings of pride, lust, revenge, love of honours, were not resisted and mourned for.

7. That my charity was cold.

8. That the experience I had of God's hearing me, in this and the other particular, being gathered, yet in a new trouble I had always (once at least) my faith to seek, as if I were to begin at A, B, C, again.

9. That I have not more boldly contradicted the enemies speaking against the truth, either in public church-meet-

ings, or at tables, or ordinary conference.

10. That in great troubles, I have received false reports of Christ's love, and misbelieved him in his chastening; whereas the event hath said that all was in mercy.

11. Nothing more moveth me, and burdeneth my soul, than that I could never, in my prosperity, so wrestle in prayer with God, nor be so dead to the world, so hungry and sick of love for Christ, so heavenly-minded, as when ten stone-weight of a heavy cross was upon me.

12. That the cross extorted vows of new obedience, which ease hath blown away, as chaff before the wind.

13. That practice was so short and narrow, and light so long and broad.

14. That death hath not been often meditated upon.

15. That I have not been careful of gaining others to Christ.

16. That my grace and gifts bring forth little or no thankfulness.

There are some things also, whereby I have been helped. As,

1. I have benefited by riding alone a long journey, in giving that time to prayer.

2. By abstinence, and giving days to God.

3. By praying for others; for, by making an errand to God for them, I have gotten something for myself.

4. I have been really confirmed, in many particulars, that God heareth prayers; and therefore I used to pray for any thing, of how little importance soever.

5. He enabled me to make no question that this way, which is mocked and nick-named, is the only way to heaven.

Sir, these and many more occurrences in my life, should be looked unto: and,

1. Thoughts of atheism should be watched over, as, 'If there be a God in heaven', which will trouble and assault the best at some times.

2. Growth in grace should be cared for above all things; and falling from our first love mourned for.

3. Conscience made of praying for the enemies, who are blinded.

Sir, I thank you most kindly for your care of my brother, and me also: I hope it is laid up for you, and remembered in heaven. I am still ashamed with Christ's kindness to such a sinner as I am. He hath left a fire in my heart that hell cannot cast water on, to quench or extinguish it. Help me to praise, and pray for me; for you have a prisoner's blessing and prayers. Remember my love to our ywife. Grace be with you.

28/TO LADY BOYD

Lessons learned in the school of adversity

Aberdeen, 1 May 1637

Madam:

Grace, mercy and peace from God our Father, and from our Lord Jesus Christ, be multiplied upon you. I have reasoned with your son[1] at large. I rejoice to see him set his face in the right airth,[2] now when the nobles love the sunny-side of the gospel best, and are afraid that Christ wants soldiers, and shall not be able to do for himself.

Madam, our debts of obligation to Christ are not small; the freedom of grace and salvation is the wonder of man and angels; but mercy in our Lord scorneth hire. You are bound to lift Christ on high, who hath given you eyes to discern the devil, now coming out in white, and the idolatry and apostasy of the time, well washed with fair pretences; but the skin is black, and the water foul. It were art, I confess, to wash

[1]Lord Boyd. [2]Quarter of the heavens, direction.

a black devil and make him white. I am in strange ups and downs, and seven times a day I lose ground. I am put often to swimming, and again my feet are set on the Rock that is higher than myself. He hath now let me see four things I never saw before.

1. The supper must be great cheer, that is up in the great hall, with the royal King of Glory, when the four-hours,[1] the standing drink,[2] in this dreary wilderness, is so sweet. When he comforteth afar off his poor heart-broken mourners in Zion, and sendeth me but his hearty commendations till we meet, I am confounded with wonder, to think what it shall be, when the fairest among the sons of men shall lay a King's sweet soft cheek to the sinful cheeks of poor sinners. O time, time, go swiftly, and hasten that day! sweet Lord Jesus, post! come flying, like a young hart or a roe upon the mountains of separation. I think we should tell the hours carefully, and look often how low the sun is: for love hath no bounds; it is pained, pained in itself, till it come into grips with the party beloved.

2. I find Christ's absence to be love's sickness and love's death. The wind that bloweth out of the airth[3] where my Lord Jesus reigneth, is sweet-smelled, soft, joyful, and heartsome to a soul burnt with absence. It is a painful battle for a soul sick of love to fight with absence and delays. Christ's 'not yet' is a stounding[4] of all the joints of the soul. A nod of his head, when he is under a mask, would be half a pledge. To say, 'Fool, what aileth thee? He is coming', would be life to a dead man. I am often, in my dumb Sabbaths, seeking a new plea with my Lord Jesus (God forgive me!), and I care not if there be not two or three ounceweight of black wrath in my cup.

3. For the third thing: I have seen my abominable vileness.

---

[1]See *p* 60 *fn* 2. [2]That is, the refreshment supplied at the house door.
[3]See *p* 73 *fn* 2. [4]An overpowering stroke that produces faintness.

If I were well known, there would none in this kingdom ask how I do. Men take my ten to be a hundred; but I am a deeper hypocrite and shallower professor than every one believeth. God knoweth I feign not. But I think my reckonings on the one page written in great letters, and his mercy to such a forlorn and wretched bankrupt on the other, more than a miracle. If I could get my finger-ends upon a full assurance, I think I should grip fast: but my cup wanteth not gall. And upon my part, despair might be almost excused, if every one in this land saw my inner-side. But I know that I am one of those who have made great sale and a free market to free grace. If I could be saved, as I would fain believe, sure I am that I have given Christ's blood, his free grace and the bowels of his mercy a large field to work upon. And Christ hath manifested his art, I dare not say to the uttermost (for he can, if he would, forgive all the devils and condemned reprobates, in respect of the wideness of his mercy), but I say to an admirable degree.

4. I am stricken with fear of unthankfulness. This apostate kirk hath played the harlot with many lovers; they are spitting in the face of my lovely King, and mocking him, and I cannot mend it; and they are running away from Christ in troops, and I cannot mourn and be grieved for it. I think Christ lieth like an old unused castle, forsaken of the inhabitants: all men run away now from him. Truth, innocent truth, goeth mourning and wringing her hands in sackcloth and ashes. Woe, woe, woe is me, for the virgin-daughter of Scotland. Woe, woe to the inhabitants of this land! for they are gone back with a perpetual backsliding. These things take me so up, that a borrowed bed, another man's fire-side, the wind upon my face, I (being driven from my lovers, and dear acquaintance, and my poor flock) find no room in my sorrow; I have no spare or odd sorrow for these: only I think the sparrows

and swallows, that build their nests in the kirk of Anwoth, blessed birds.

Nothing hath given my faith a harder back-set, till it crack again, than my closed mouth. But let me be miserable myself alone; God keep my dear brethren from it. But still I keep breath. And when my royal, and never, never-enough-praised King returneth to his sinful prisoner, I ride upon the high places of Jacob, I divide Shechem, I triumph in his strength. If this kingdom would glorify the Lord in my behalf! I desire to be weighed in God's even balance in this point, if I think not my wages paid to the full. I shall crave no more hire of Christ.

Madam, pity me in this, and help me to praise him: for whatever I be, the chief of sinners, a devil, and a most guilty devil, yet it is the apple of Christ's eye, his honour and glory as the Head of the church, that I suffer for now, and that I will go to eternity with. I am greatly in love with Mr M. M.[1] I see him stamped with the image of God. I hope well of your son, my Lord Boyd. Your Ladyship and your children have a prisoner's prayers. Grace, grace be with you.

29/TO JOHN STUART

Commercial misfortunes
Service-Book
Blessedness of trials

Aberdeen, 1637

Much honoured Sir:
Grace, mercy and peace be unto you. I long to hear from you, being now removed from my flock, and the prisoner of

[1]Matthew Mowat, minister of Kilmarnock. See Letter 41.

Christ at Aberdeen. I would not have you to think it strange that your journey to New England hath gotten such a dash. It indeed hath made my heart heavy; yet I know it is no dumb Providence, but a speaking one, whereby our Lord speaketh his mind to you, though for the present ye do not well understand what he saith. However it be, he who sitteth upon the floods hath shown you his marvellous loving kindness in the great depths. I know that your loss is great, and your hope is gone far against you. But I entreat you, Sir, expound aright our Lord's laying all hindrances in the way. I persuade myself that your heart aimeth at the footsteps of the flock, to feed beside the shepherds' tents, and to dwell beside him whom your soul loveth; and that it is your desire to remain in the wilderness where the Woman is kept from the Dragon [*Rev* 12. 14]. And this being your desire, remember that a poor prisoner of Christ said it to you, that that miscarried journey is with child to you of mercy and consolation, and shall bring forth a fair birth on which the Lord will attend. Wait on: 'He that believeth maketh not haste' [*Is* 28. 16].

I hope that you have been asking what the Lord meaneth, and what further may be his will, in reference to your return. My dear brother, let God make of you what he will, he will end all with consolation, and will make glory out of your sufferings; and would you wish better work? This water was in your way to heaven and written in your Lord's book: ye behoved to cross it, and therefore, kiss his wise and unerring Providence. Let not the censures of men, who see but the outside of things, and scarce well that, abate your courage and rejoicing in the Lord. Howbeit your faith seeth but the black side of Providence, yet it hath a better side, and God will let you see it.

Learn to believe Christ better than his strokes; himself and his promises better than his glooms.[1] Dashes and disappoint-

[1] See p 67 *fn* 3.

ments are not canonical Scripture. Fighting for the promised
land seemed to cry to God's promise, 'Thou liest'. If our
Lord ride upon a straw, his horse shall neither stumble nor
fall. 'For we know that all things work together for good to
them that love God' [*Rom* 8. 28]. *Ergo*, shipwreck, losses, etc.
work together for the good of them that love God. Hence I
infer that losses, disappointments, ill-tongues, loss of friends,
houses or country, are God's workmen, set on work to work
out good to you, out of everything that befalleth you. Let
not the Lord's dealing seem harsh, rough, or unfatherly
because it is unpleasant. When the Lord's blessed will bloweth
across your desires, it is best, in humility, to strike sail to him,
and to be willing to be led any way our Lord pleaseth. It is a
point of denial of yourself, to be as if you had not a will,
but had made a free disposition of it to God, and had sold it
over to him. And to make use of his will for your own is
both true holiness, and your ease and peace. You know not
what the Lord is working out of this, but you shall know it
hereafter.

And what I write to you I write to your wife. I compas-
sionate her case but entreat her not to fear nor faint. This
journey is a part of her wilderness to heaven and the promised land, and there are fewer miles behind. It is nearer the
dawning of the day to her than when she went out of Scotland. I should be glad to hear that you and she have comfort
and courage in the Lord.

Now as concerning our kirk; our Service-Book is ordained,
by open proclamation and sound of trumpet, to be read in
all the kirks of the kingdom.[1] Our prelates are to meet this
month about our Canons, and for a reconciliation betwixt
us and the Lutherans. The Professors of Aberdeen University
are charged to draw up the Articles of an uniform Confession;

[1] It was the reading of 'Laud's Liturgy' in St Giles' Cathedral, Edinburgh, that
caused Jenny Geddes the herb-stall woman to throw her stool at the Dean's
head. The attempt to foist Episcopacy on Scotland led to the signing of the
National Covenant in 1638 and to the two Bishops' wars 1639-40.

but reconciliation with Popery is intended. This is the day of Jacob's visitation; the ways of Zion mourn, our gold is become dim, the sun is gone down upon our prophets. A dry wind, but neither to fan nor to cleanse, is coming upon this land; and all our ill is coming from the multiplied transgressions of this land and from the friends and lovers of Babel among us. 'The violence done to me and to my flesh be upon Babylon, shall the inhabitant of Zion say; and, my blood upon the inhabitants of Chaldea, shall Jerusalem say' [*Jer* 51. 35].

Now for myself: I was three days before the High Commission, and accused of treason preached against our King. (A minister being witness, went well nigh to swear it). God hath saved me from their malice.

Firstly, they have deprived me of my ministry;

Secondly, Silenced me, that I exercise no part of the ministerial function within this kingdom, under the pain of rebellion;

Thirdly, Confined my person within the town of Aberdeen, where I find the ministers working for my confinement in Caithness or Orkney, far from them, because some people here (willing to be edified) resort to me.

At my first entry I had heavy challenges within me, and a court fenced (but I hope not in Christ's name), wherein it was asserted that my Lord would have no more of my services and was tired of me. And like a fool I summoned Christ also for unkindness. My soul fainted and I refused comfort, and said, 'What ailed Christ at me? for I desired to be faithful in his house'. Thus, in my rovings and mistakings, my Lord Jesus bestowed mercy on me, who am less than the least of all saints. I lay upon the dust, and bought a plea from Satan against Christ, and he was content to sell it. But at length Christ did show himself friends with me, and in mercy pardoned and passed my part of it, and only complained that a court should be holden in his bounds without his allowance.

Now I pass from my compearance;[1] and as if Christ had done the fault, he hath made the mends and returned to my soul. So that now his poor prisoner feedeth on the feasts of love.

My adversaries know not what a courtier I am now with my Royal King for whose crown I now suffer. It is but our soft and lazy flesh that hath raised an ill report of the cross of Christ. O sweet, sweet is his yoke! Christ's chains are of pure gold; sufferings for him are perfumed. I would not give my weeping for the laughing of all the fourteen prelates; I would not exchange my sadness with the world's joy. O lovely, lovely Jesus, how sweet must thy kisses be when thy cross smelleth so sweetly! Oh, if all the three kingdoms had part of my love-feast and of the comfort of a dawted[2] prisoner!

Dear brother, I charge you to praise for me, and to seek help of our acquaintance there to help me to praise. Why should I smother Christ's honesty to me? My heart is taken up with this, that my silence and sufferings may preach. I beseech you in the bowels of Christ to help me to praise. Remember my love to your wife, to Mr Blair and Mr Livingstone and Mr Cunningham. Let me hear from you, for I am anxious what to do. If I saw a call for New England I would follow it. Grace be with you.

Appearance in court.
[2] See p 54 *fn* 3.

30/TO DAVID DICKSON

Christ's infinite fulness

Aberdeen, 1 May 1637

My Reverend and dear Brother:

I fear that you have never known me well. If you saw my inner side, it is possible that you would pity me, but you would hardly give me either love or respect. Men mistake me the whole length of the heavens. My sins prevail over me, and the terrors of their guiltiness. I am put often to ask if Christ and I did ever shake hands together in earnest. I mean not that my feast-days are quite gone, but I am made of extremes. I pray God that you never have the woeful and dreary experience of a closed mouth, for then you shall judge the sparrows, that may sing on the church of Irvine, blessed birds. But my soul hath been refreshed and watered, when I hear of your courage and zeal for your never-enough-praised, praised Master, in that you put the men of God, chased out of Ireland, to work. O if I could confirm you! I dare say, in God's presence, that this shall never hasten your suffering, but will be David Dickson's feast and sparkling joy, that while he had time and leisure he put many to work, to lift up Jesus, his sweet Master, high in the skies. O man of God, go on, go on. Be valiant for that Plant of renown, for that Chief among ten thousands, for that Prince of the kings of the earth. It is but little that I know of God; yet this I dare write, that Christ will be glorified in David Dickson, howbeit Scotland be not gathered.

I am pained, pained, that I have not more to give my sweet Bridegroom. His comforts to me are not dealt with a niggard's hand; but I would fain learn not to idolize comfort, sense, joy, and sweet felt presence. All these are but creatures and nothing but the kingly robe, the gold ring, and the bracelets of the Bridegroom. The Bridegroom himself is better than all the ornaments that are about him. Now, I would not so much have these as God himself, and to be swallowed up of love to Christ. I see that in delighting in a communion with Christ we may make more gods than one. But, however, all was but bairns' play between Christ and me till now. If one would have sworn unto me, I would not have believed what may be found in Christ. I hope that you pity my pain that much, in my prison, as to help me yourself, and to cause others help me, a dyvour,[1] a sinful wretched dyvour,[1] to pay some of my debts of praise to my great King. Let my God be judge and witness, if my soul would not have sweet ease and comfort, to have many hearts confirmed in Christ, and enlarged with his love, and many tongues set on work to set on high my royal and princely Well-beloved. O that my sufferings could pay tribute to such a King!

I have given over wondering at his love, for Christ hath manifested a piece of art upon me, that I never revealed to any living. He hath gotten fair and rich employment, and sweet sale, and a goodly market for his honourable calling of showing mercy, on me the chief of sinners. Every one knoweth not so well as I do my woefully-often broken covenants. My sins against light, working in the very act of sinning, have been met with admirable mercy. But alas! He will get nothing back again but wretched unthankfulness. I am sure that if Christ pity anything in me next to my sin, it is pain of love for an armful and soulful of himself, in faith, love, and begun fruition. My sorrow is that I cannot get Christ lifted off the dust in Scotland, and set on high, above all the skies and heaven of heavens.

[1]See p 59 *fn* 1.

31/TO JOHN CLARK

Marks of difference betwixt Christians and reprobates

Aberdeen [undated]

Loving Brother:

Hold fast Christ without wavering, and contend for the faith, because Christ is not easily gotten nor kept. The lazy professor hath put heaven as it were at the very next door and thinketh to fly up to heaven in his bed, and in a night-dream. But truly, that is not so easy a thing as most men believe. Christ himself did sweat ere he won this city, howbeit he was the freeborn heir. It is Christianity, my heart, to be sincere, unfeigned honest, and upright-hearted before God, and to live and serve God, suppose there was not one man nor woman in all the world dwelling beside you, to eye you. Any little grace that you have, see that it be sound and true.

You may put a difference betwixt you and reprobates, if you have these marks:

1. If ye prize Christ and his truth so as you will sell all and buy him, and suffer for it.
2. If the love of Christ keepeth you back from sinning, more than the law, or fear of hell.
3. If you be humble and deny your own will, wit, credit, ease, honour, the world, and the vanity and glory of it.
4. Your profession must not be barren and void of good works.
5. You must in all things aim at God's honour. You must eat, drink, sleep, buy, sell, sit, stand, speak, pray, read, and hear the Word, with a heart-purpose that God may be honoured.

6. You must show yourself an enemy to sin, and reprove the works of darkness, such as drunkenness, swearing, and lying, albeit the company should hate you for so doing.

7. Keep in mind the truth of God that you heard me teach, and have nothing to do with the corruptions and new guises entering into the house of God.

8. Make conscience of your calling, in covenants, in buying and selling.

9. Acquaint yourself with daily praying; commit all your ways and actions to God by prayer, supplication, and thanksgiving. And count not much of being mocked, for Christ Jesus was mocked before you.

Persuade yourself that this is the way of peace and comfort which I now suffer for. I dare go to death and into eternity with it, though men may possibly see another way. Remember me in your prayers, and the state of this oppressed church. Grace be with you.

32/TO EARLSTON, YOUNGER

Dangers of youth
Christ the best Physician
Four remedies against doubting
Breathing after Christ's honour

Aberdeen, 16 June 1637

Much honoured and well-beloved in the Lord:

Grace, mercy and peace be to you. Your letters give a dash to my laziness in writing. I must first tell you that there is not such a glassy, icy, and slippery piece of way betwixt you and heaven, as youth. I have experience to say with me here, and seal what I assert. The old ashes of the sins of my youth are new fire of sorrow to me. I have seen the devil, as it were, dead and buried, and yet rise again, and be a worse devil than ever he was. Therefore, my brother, beware of a green young devil, that hath never been buried: the devil in his flowers (I mean the hot fiery lusts and passions of youth) is much to be feared; for in youth he findeth dry sticks and dry coals, and a hot hearth-stone. And how soon can he with his flint cast fire, and with his bellows blow it up, and fire the house! Sanctified thoughts, thoughts made conscience of, and called in, and kept in awe, are green fuel that burn not, and are a water for Satan's coal. Yet I must tell you, all the saints now triumphant in heaven, and standing before the throne, are nothing but Christ's forlorn and beggarly bankrupts. What are they but a pack of redeemed sinners? But their redemption is not only past the seals, but completed; and yours is on the wheels and in doing. All Christ's good bairns go to heaven with a broken brow, and with a crooked leg. Christ hath an advantage of you; and I pray you let him have it; he shall find employment for his calling in you. If it were not with you as you write, grace should find no sale nor market in you; but you must be content to give Christ somewhat to do. I am glad that he is employed that way. Let your bleeding soul and your sores be put in the hand of this expert Physician. Let young and strong corruptions and his free grace be yoked together, and let Christ and your sins deal it betwixt them.

I shall be loath to put you off your fears, and your sense of deadness; I wish it were more. There are some wounds whose bleeding should not be soon stopped. You must take a house beside the Physician. It will be a miracle if you be the first sick man whom he put away uncured, and worse than he found you. Nay, nay, Christ is honest, and in that sinners have nothing to say against him. 'And him that cometh to me, I will in no wise cast out' [*John* 6. 37]. Take that: it cannot be presumption to take that as your own, when you find your wounds stound[1] you. Presumption is ever whole at the heart, and hath but the truant-sickness, and groaneth only for the fashion. Faith hath sense of sickness, and looketh like a friend to the promises; and looking to Christ therein, is glad to see a known face.

Christ is as full a feast as you can have to hunger for. Nay, Christ, I say, is not a full man's leavings. His mercy sends always a letter of defiance to all your sins, if there were ten thousand more of them. I grant you that it is a hard matter for a poor hungry man to win his meat upon a hidden Christ; for then the key of his pantry door, and of the house of wine, is to be sought, and cannot be had; but hunger must break through iron locks. I bemoan them not who can make a din and ado for a lost Saviour. You must let him hear it (to say so) upon both sides of his head, when he hideth himself; it is no time then to be bird-mouthed[2] and patient. Christ is rare indeed, and precious to a sinner; he is a miracle, and a world's wonder to a seeking and a weeping sinner! but yet such a miracle as shall be seen by them who will come and see. The seeker and sigher is at last a singer and enjoyer; nay, I have seen a dumb man get an alms from Christ. He that can tell his tale, and send such a letter to heaven as he hath sent to Aberdeen, is very likely to speed with Christ; it bodeth God's mercy to complain heartily for sin. Let wrestling be with Christ till he say, 'How is it, sir, that I cannot be quit of your bills and your misleared[3] cries?' And then hope for Christ's blessing; and his blessing is better than ten other blessings.

Be not ashamed because of your guiltiness; necessity must not blush to beg. It standeth you hard to want Christ, and therefore, that which idle on-waiting cannot do, misnurtured crying, and knocking will do. And for doubtings, because you are not as you were long since with your Master, consider three things:

[1] See *p* 74 *fn* 4.
[2] Mealy-mouthed.   [3] Rude, uncouth.

1. What if Christ had such tottering thoughts of the bargain of the new covenant, betwixt you and him, as you have?
2. Your heart is not the compass Christ saileth by. He will give you leave to sing as you please, but he will not dance to your daft spring.[1] It is not referred to you and your thoughts, what Christ will do with the charters betwixt you and him. Your own misbelief hath torn them, but he hath the principal in heaven with himself. Your thoughts are no parts of the new covenant; dreams change not Christ.
3. Doubtings are your sins, but they are Christ's drugs and ingredients that the Physician maketh use of for the curing of your pride. Is it not suitable for a beggar to say at meat, 'God reward the winners'?[2] for then he saith that he knoweth who beareth the charges of the house. It is also meet you should know by experience, that faith is not nature's ill-gotten bastard, but your Lord's free gift, that lay in the womb of God's free grace. Praised be the winner! I may add,
4. In the passing of your bill and your charters, when they went through the Mediator's great seal, and were concluded, faith's advice was not sought. Faith hath not a vote beside Christ's merits: blood, blood, dear blood, that came from your Surety's holy body, maketh that sure work.

The use then which you have of faith now (having already closed with Jesus Christ for justification) is, to take out a copy of your pardon; and so you have peace with God, upon the account of Christ. For, since faith apprehendeth pardon, but never payeth a penny for it, no marvel that salvation doth not die and live, ebb or flow, with the working of faith. But, because it is for your Lord's honour to believe his mercy and his fidelity, it is infinite goodness in our Lord that misbelief giveth a dash to our Lord's glory, and not to our salvation.

[1] Tune.
[2] That is, 'those who got this meat for us'.

And so, whoever want, (yea although God here bear with the want of what we are obliged to give him, even the glory of his grace, by believing), yet a poor covenanted sinner wanteth not. But if guiltiness were removed, doubtings would find no friend nor life; and yet faith is to believe the removal of guiltiness in Christ. A reason why you get less now, as you think, than before (as I take it) is, because, at our first conversion, our Lord putteth the meat in young bairns' mouths with his own hand; but when we grow to some further perfection, we must take heaven by violence, and take by violence from Christ what we get. And he can, and doth hold, because he will have us to draw. Remember now that you must live upon violent plucking. Laziness is a greater fault now than long since. We love always to have the pap put into our mouth.

Now for myself. Alas! I am not the man I go for in this nation; men have not just weights to weigh me in. O, but I am a silly feckless[1] body, and over-grown with weeds; corruption is rank and fat in me. O that I were answerable to this holy cause, and to that honourable Prince's love, for whom I now suffer! If Christ were to refer the matter to me (in his presence I speak it), I might be ashamed to vote my own salvation. I think Christ might say, 'Art thou not ashamed to claim heaven, who dost so little for it?' I am very often so, that I know not whether I sink or swim in the water; I find myself a bag of light froth. I could bear no weight (but vanities and nothings weigh in Christ's balance) if my Lord cast not in borrowed weight and metal, even Christ's righteousness, to weigh for me. The stock I have is not mine own; I am but the merchant who trafficketh with other folks' goods. If my creditor, Christ, would take from me what he hath lent, I could not long keep the causeway; but Christ hath made it mine and his. I think it manhood to play the coward

[1] See p 40 *fn* 1.

and jouk[1] in the lee-side of Christ. Thus I am not only saved from my enemies, but I obtain the victory. I am so empty, that I think it were an alms-deed in Christ, if he would win a poor prisoner's blessing for evermore, and fill me with his love.

I complain that when Christ cometh, he cometh always to fetch fire, he is ever in haste, he may not tarry; and poor I get but a standing visit, and but, 'How doest thou?' in the by-going. I dare not say he is lordly, because he is made a King now at the right-hand of God; or is grown miskenning[2] and dry to his poor friends. But I think it my happiness to love the love of Christ; and when he goeth away, the memory of his sweet presence is like a feast in a dear summer. I have comfort in this, that my soul desireth that every hour of my imprisonment were a company of heavenly tongues, to praise him on my behalf, howbeit my bonds were prolonged for many hundred years. O that I could be the man who could procure my Lord's glory to flow like a full sea, and blow like a mighty wind upon all the four airths[3] of Scotland, England, and Ireland. O if I could write a book of his praises!

O Fairest among the sons of men, why stayest thou so long away? O heavens, move fast! O time, run, run, and hasten the marriage-day! for love is tormented with delays. O angels, O seraphim who stand before him, O blessed spirits who now see his face, set him on high! for when you have worn your harps in his praises, all is too little, and is nothing, to cast the smell of the praise of that fair flower, that fragrant Rose of Sharon, through many worlds! Sir, take my hearty commendations to him and tell him that I am sick of love. Grace be with you.

---

[1]Shrink from and avoid danger.   [2]That is, as if he overlooked them.
[3]See *p 73 fn 2.*

33/TO WILLIAM DALGLEISH

Fragrance of the ministry
Review of past and present situation, and of future prospects

Aberdeen, 16 June 1637

Reverend and well-beloved Brother:

Grace, mercy and peace be unto you. I have heard somewhat of your trials in Galloway. I bless the Lord, who hath begun first in that corner to make you a new kirk to himself. Christ hath the less ado behind, when he hath refined you.

Let me entreat you, my dearly beloved, to be fast to Christ. My witness is above, my dearest brother, that you have added much joy to me in my bonds, when I hear that you grow in the grace and zeal of God for your Master. Our ministry, whether by preaching or by suffering, will cast a smell through the world both of heaven and hell [2 *Cor* 2. 15, 16]. I persuade you, my dear brother, that there is nothing out of heaven, next to Christ, dearer to me than my ministry; and the worth of it, in my estimation, is swelled, and paineth me exceedingly. Yet I am content, for the honour of my Lord, to surrender it back again to the Lord of the vineyard. Let him do with it, and me both, what he thinketh good. I think myself too little for him.

And, let me speak to you, how kind a fellow-prisoner is Christ to me! Believe me, this kind of cross (that would not go by my door, but would needs visit me) is still the longer the more welcome to me. It is true, my silent Sabbaths have been, and still are, as glassy ice whereon my faith can scarce hold its feet, and I am often blown on my back and off my feet with a storm of doubting. Yet truly, my bonds all this time cast a mighty and rank smell of high and deep love in

Christ. I cannot, indeed, see through my cross to the far end; yet I believe I am in Christ's books, and in his decree (not yet unfolded to me), a man triumphing, dancing and singing on the other side of the Red Sea, and laughing and praising the Lamb, over beyond time, sorrow, deprivation, prelates' indignation, losses, want of friends, and death. Heaven is not a fowl flying in the air (as men used to speak of things that are uncertain); nay, it is well paid for. Christ's comprisement lieth on glory[1] for all the mourners in Zion, and shall never be loosed. Let us be glad and rejoice that we have blood, losses and wounds to show our Master and Captain at his appearance, and what we suffered for his cause.

Woe is me, my dear brother, that I say often, 'I am but dry bones which my Lord will not bring out of the grave again', and that my faithless fears say, 'O, I am a dry tree that can bear no fruit; I am a useless body who can beget no children to the Lord in his house!' Hopes of deliverance look cold and uncertain, and afar off, as if I had done with it. It is much for Christ (if I may say so) to get law-borrows[2] of my sorrow and of my quarrelous[3] heart. Christ's love playeth me fair play. I am not wronged at all; but there is a tricking and false heart within me that still playeth Christ foul play. I am a cumbersome neighbour to Christ: it is a wonder that he dwelleth beside the like of me. Yet I often get the advantage of the hill above my temptations, and then I despise temptation, even hell itself, and the stink of it, and the instruments of it, and am proud of my honourable Master. And I resolve, whether contrary winds will or not, to fetch[4] Christ's harbour; and I think a wilful and stiff contention with my Lord Jesus for his love very lawful.

It is sometimes hard to me to win my meat upon Christ's love, because my faith is sick and my hope withereth and my eyes wax dim; and unkind and comfort-eclipsing clouds go

---

[1] That is, Christ sees to it that the mourners in Zion are secured in possession of glory.   [2] Pledges not to injure (Christ's cause).   [3] Fault-finding.
[4] Reach.

over the fair and bright Sun, Jesus. And then, when I and temptation tryst the matter together, we spill all through unbelief. Sweet, sweet for evermore would my life be if I could keep faith in exercise! But I see that my fire cannot always cast light. I have even a 'poor man's hard world' when he goeth away. But surely, since my entry hither, many a time hath my fair sun shined without a cloud. Hot and burning hath Christ's love been to me. I have no vent to the expression of it; I must be content with stolen and smothered desires of Christ's glory. O how far is his love behind the hand with me![1] I am just like a man who hath nothing to pay his thousands of debt. All that can be gotten of him is to seize upon his person. Except Christ would seize upon my-self, and make the readiest payment that can be of my heart and love to himself, I have no other thing to give him. If my sufferings could do beholders good, and edify his kirk, and proclaim the incomparable worth of Christ's love to the world, O then would my soul be overjoyed and my sad heart be cheered and calmed!

Dear brother, I cannot tell what is become of my labours among that people. If all that my Lord builded by me be casten down, and the bottom be fallen out of the profession of that parish, and none stand by Christ whose love I once preached as clearly and plainly as I could (though far below its worth and excellence) to that people – if so, how can I bear it! And if another make a foul harvest, where I have made a painful and honest sowing, it will not soon digest with me. But I know that his ways pass finding out. Yet my witness, both within me and above me, knoweth. And my pained breast upon the Lord's Day at night, my desire to have had Christ awful and amiable and sweet to that people, is now my joy. It was my desire and aim to make Christ and them one; and if I see my hope die in the bud, ere they bloom a little and come to no fruit, I die with grief.

[1] That is, his love is far from receiving what I owe to it.

O my God, seek not an account of the violence done to me by my brethren, whose salvation I love and desire. I pray that they and I be not heard as contrary parties in the day of our compearance[1] before our Judge, in that process, led by them against my ministry which I received from Christ. I know that a little inch, and less than the third part of this span-length and hand-breadth of time which is posting away, will put me without the stroke, and above the reach, of either brethren or foes; and it is a short-lasting injury done to me and to my pains in that part of my Lord's vineyard. O how silly[2] an advantage is my deprivation to me, seeing that my Lord Jesus hath many ways to recover his own losses, and is irresistible to compass his own glorious ends, that his lily may grow amongst thorns, and his little kingdom exalt itself, even under the swords and spears of contrary powers!

But, my dear brother, go on in the strength of his rich grace, whom ye serve. Stand fast for Christ. Deliver the Gospel off your hand, and your ministry to your Master, with a clean and undefiled conscience. Loose not a pin of Christ's tabernacle. Do not so much as pick with your nail at one board or border of the ark. Have no part or dealing, upon any terms, in a hoof [*Exod* 10. 26], in a closed window [*Dan* 6. 10], or in a bowing of your knee, in casting down of the temple. But be a mourning and speaking witness against them who now ruin Zion. Our Master will be on us all now in a clap, ere ever we wit. That day will discover all our whites and our blacks concerning this controversy of poor oppressed Zion. Let us make our part of it good, that it may be able to abide the fire, when hay and stubble shall be burned to ashes. Nothing, nothing, I say, nothing but sound sanctification can abide the Lord's fan. I stand to my testimony that I preached often of Scotland – 'Lamentation, mourning and woe abideth thee, O Scotland! O Scotland! the fearful quarrel of a broken covenant standeth good with thy Lord!'

[1]See *p* 80 *fn* 1. [2]Poor, frail.

Now, remember my love to all my friends and to my parishioners, as if I named each of them particularly. I recommend you and God's people, committed by Christ to your trust, to the rich grace of our all-sufficient Lord. Remember my bonds. Praise my Lord, who beareth me up in my sufferings. As you find occasion, according to the wisdom given you, show our acquaintance what the Lord hath done for my soul. This I seek not, verily, to hunt my own praise, but that my sweetest and dearest Master may be magnified in my sufferings.

34/TO JOHN STUART

Hope for Scotland
Self-submission
Christ himself sought by faith
Stability of salvation
Christ's ways

Aberdeen, 1637

Worthy Sir:

Grace, mercy and peace be with you. I long for the time when I shall see the beauty of the Lord in his house; and would be as glad of it as of any sight on earth, to see the halt, the blind, and the lame come back to Zion with supplications [*Jer* 31. 8, 9]. 'Going and weeping, and seeking the Lord, asking their way to Zion, with their faces thitherward' [*Jer* 50. 4, 5]; and to see the woman travailing in birth, delivered of the man-child *of a blessed reformation*.

If this land were humbled, I would look that our skies should clear, and our day dawn again; and you should then bless Christ, who is content to save your travail, and to give himself to you, in pure ordinances, on this side of the sea. I know the mercy of Christ is engaged by promise to Scotland, notwithstanding he bring wrath, as I fear he will, upon this land. I am waiting on for enlargement, and half content that my faith bow, if Christ, while he bow it, keep it unbroken; for who goeth through a fire without a mark or a scald? I see the Lord making use of this fire to scour his vessels from their rust. O that my will were silent, and as 'a child weaned from the breasts!' [*Psalm* 131. 2]. But, alas! who hath a heart that will give Christ the last word in the contest, and will hear, and not speak again? Oh! contests and querulous replies, as 'I do well to be angry, even unto death' [*Jonah* 4. 9], smell of the stink of strong corruption. Oh, blessed soul, that could sacrifice his will, and go to heaven, having lost his will and made resignation of it to Christ! I would seek no more but that Christ were absolute king over my will, and that my will were a sufferer in all crosses, without meeting Christ with such a word, 'Why is it thus?' I wish still that my love had but leave to stand beside beautiful Jesus, and to get the mercy of looking to him, and burning for him, suppose that possession of him were suspended till my Lord fold together the leaves and two sides of the little shepherds' tents of clay.

Oh what pain is there in longing for Christ, under an overclouded and eclipsed assurance! What is harder than to burn, pine with longing and deaths of love, and then to have blanks and uninked paper for[1] assurance of Christ in real fruition or possession? Oh how sweet were one line or half a letter of a written assurance under Christ's own hand! But this is our exercise daily, that guilt shall overmist and darken assurance. It is a miracle to believe, but for a sinner to believe is two miracles. But oh, what obligations of love are we under to Christ, who beareth with our wild apprehensions, in suffering them to nick-name sweet Jesus, and to put a lie upon

[1]That is, instead of.

his good name! If he had not been God, and if long-suffering in Christ were not like Christ himself, we should long ago have broken Christ's mercies in two pieces, and put an iron-bar upon our own salvation, that mercy should not have been able to break or over-leap. But long-suffering in God is God himself; and that is our salvation; and the stability of our heaven is in God.

He who said, 'Christ in you the hope of glory' [*Col* 1. 27], (for our hope and the foundation and pillars of it is Christ-God) knew that sinners are anchor-fast and made stable in God; so that if God do not change, which is impossible, then my hope shall not fluctuate. O sweet stability of well-founded salvation! Who could win heaven, if this were not so? and who could be saved, if God were not God, and if he were not such a God as he is? O, God be thanked, that our salvation is coasted and landed and shored upon Christ, who is Master of winds and storms! And what sea-winds can blow the coast or the land out of its place? Bulwarks are often cast down, but coasts are not removed; but suppose that were or might be, yet God cannot reel nor remove.

Oh that we should go from this strong and unmoveable Lord, and that we should loosen ourselves, if it were in our power, from him! Alas, our green and young love hath not taken with Christ, being unacquainted with him. He is such a wide and broad, deep and high, and surpassing sweetness, that our love is too little for him; but oh that our love, little as it is, could unite with his great and huge sweetness and transcendent excellency! O thrice blessed, and eternally blessed are they who are out of themselves, that they may be in love united to him!

I am often rolling up and down the thoughts of my faint and sick desires of expressing Christ's glory before his people. But I see not through the throng of impediments, and cannot find eyes to look higher; and so I put many things in Christ's way to hinder him, that I know he would but laugh at, and with one stride set his foot over them all. I know not if my Lord will bring me to his sanctuary or not; but I know he hath the placing of me either within or without the house, and that nothing will be done without him. But I am often thinking and saying within myself, that my days flee away, and I see no good, neither yet Christ's work thriving; and it is likely the grave shall prevent[1] the answer of my desires of saving of souls as I would. But alas! I cannot make right work of his ways. I neither spell nor read my Lord's providence aright. My thoughts go away, so that I fear they meet not God; for it is likely God will not come the way of my thoughts. And I cannot be taught to crucify to him my wisdom and desires, and to make him King over my thoughts; for I would have a princedom over my thoughts, and would boldly and blindly prescribe to God, and guide myself in a way of my own making. But I hold my peace here; let him do his will. Grace, grace be with you.

35/TO EARLSTON, YOUNGER

Sufferings
Hope of final deliverance
The believer in safe keeping
Dependence on Christ for perseverance

Aberdeen, 1637

Worthy and dearly beloved in the Lord:

Grace, mercy and peace be to you. I long to hear from you. I remain still a prisoner of hope, and do think it service to the Lord to wait on still with submission, till the Lord's morning sky break, and his summer day dawn. For I am

[1] Come before.

persuaded, it is a piece of the chief errand of our life, that God sent us for some years down to this earth, among devils and men, the fire-brands of the devil, and temptations, that we might suffer for a time here amongst our enemies; otherwise he might have made heaven to wait on us, at our coming out of the womb, and have carried us home to our country, without letting us set down our feet in this knotty and thorny life; but seeing a piece of suffering is carved to every one of us, less or more, as Infinite Wisdom hath thought good, our part is to harden and habituate our soft and thin-skinned nature to endure fire and water, devils, lions, men, losses, wo[1] hearts as those that are looked upon by God, angels, men and devils.

O what folly is it to sit down and weep upon a decree of God, that is both dumb and deaf at our tears, and must stand still as unmoveable as God who made it! For who can come behind our Lord, to alter or improve what he hath decreed and done? It were better to make windows in our prison, and to look out to God and our country, heaven, and to cry like fettered men, who long for the king's free air, 'Lord, let thy kingdom come, O let the Bridegroom come! And, O day, O fair day, O everlasting summer day, dawn and shine out, break out from under the black sky, and shine!'

I am persuaded that, if every day a little stone in the prison walls were broken, and thereby assurance given to the chained prisoner, lying under twenty stone of irons upon arms and legs, that at length his chain should wear in two pieces, and a hole should be made at length, as wide as he might come safely out to his long-desired liberty; he would in patience wait on, till time should hole the prison-wall and break his chains. The Lord's hopeful prisoners, under their trials, are in that case: years and months will take out, now one little stone, then another, of this house of clay, and at length time shall work out the breadth of a fair door, and

[1] Sorrowful.

send out the imprisoned soul to the free air in heaven; and time shall file off, by little and little, our iron-bolts which are now on legs and arms, and out-date and wear our troubles thread-bare, and then wear them to nothing: for what I suffered yesterday, I know, shall never come again to trouble me.

O that we could breathe out new hope, and new submission, every day, into Christ's lap! For certainly, a weight of glory well weighed, yea, increasing to a far more exceeding and eternal weight, shall recompense both weight and length of light and short-dated crosses. Our waters are but ebb, and come neither to our chin, nor to the stopping of our breath. I may see (if I would borrow eyes from Christ) dry land, and that near; why then should we not laugh at adversity, and scorn our short-born and soon-dying temptations!

I rejoice in the hope of the glory to be revealed; for it is no uncertain glory we look for. Our hope is not hung upon such an untwisted thread as, 'I imagine so,' or 'It is likely'; but the cable, the strong tow of our fastened anchor, is the oath and promise of Him who is eternal verity. Our salvation is fastened with God's own hand, and with Christ's own strength, to the strong stoup[1] of God's unchangeable nature, 'I am the Lord, I change not; therefore ye sons of Jacob are not consumed' [*Mal* 3. 6]. We may play, and dance, and leap upon our worthy and immoveable Rock; the ground is sure and good, and will abide the assaults of hell and the world.

O if our faith could ride it out, against the high and proud winds and waves, when our sea seemeth all to be on fire! O how oft do I let my grips go! I am put to swimming and hal sinking. I find that the devil hath the advantage of the ground in this battle, for he fighteth on known ground, in our corrupt nature. Alas! that is a friend near of kin and blood to himself, and will not fail to fall foul upon us. And hence it is, that he, who saveth to the uttermost, and leadeth many sons

[1]Post, prop.

to glory, is still righting my salvation.

Twenty times a-day I ravel[1] my heaven, and then I must come with my ill-ravelled work to Christ, to cumber him (as it were) to right it; and to seek again the right end of the thread, and to fold up again my eternal glory with his own hand, and to give a right cast of his holy and gracious hand to my marred and spoiled salvation. Certainly, it is a cumbersome thing to keep a foolish child from falls and broken brows, and weeping for this and that toy, and rash running and sickness, and bairns' diseases; ere he get through them all, he costeth no little care and fashery[2] to his keepers. And so is a believer a cumbersome piece of work, and an ill-ravelled hesp[3] (as we use to say) to Christ. But God be thanked; for many spoiled salvations, and many ill-ravelled hesps hath Christ mended, since first he entered tutor to lost mankind. O what could we bairns do without him! how soon should we mar all! But the less our weight be upon our own feeble legs, and the more on Christ, the strong Rock, the better for us. It is good for us that ever Christ took the cumber of us; it is our heaven to lay many weights and burdens upon Christ, and to make him all we have, root and top, beginning and ending of our salvation. Lord, hold us here.

Now to this tutor, and rich Lord, I recommend you. Hold fast till he come; and remember his prisoner. Grace, grace be with you.

---

[1] Twist the threads disorderly.
[2] Trouble about a multitude of small things.   [3] Hank of yarn.

36/TO WILLIAM GORDON [OF KENMURE]

Testimony to Christ's worth
Marks of grace in conviction of sin and spiritual conflict

Aberdeen, 1637

Dear Brother:

Grace, mercy and peace be to you. I have been long answering your letter, which came in good time to me. It is my aim and hearty desire that my furnace, which is of the Lord's kindling, may sparkle fire upon standers-by, to the warming of their hearts with God's love. The very dust that falleth from Christ's feet, His old ragged clothes, his knotty and black cross, are sweeter to me than king's golden crowns, and their time-eaten pleasures. I should be a liar and false witness, if I would not give my Lord Jesus a fair testimonial with my whole soul. My word, I know, will not heighten him; he needeth not such props under his feet to raise his glory high. But oh that I could raise him the height of heaven, and the breadth and length of ten heavens, in the estimation of all his young lovers! for we have all shapen Christ but too narrow and too short, and formed conceptions of his love, in our conceit, very unworthy of it. Oh that men were taken and catched with his beauty and fairness! they would give over playing with idols, in which there is not half room for the love of one soul to expatiate itself. And man's love is but heart-hungered in gnawing upon bare bones, and sucking at dry breasts.

It is well wared[1] they want who will not come to him who hath a world of love and goodness and bounty for all. We seek to thaw our frozen hearts at the cold smoke of the short-timed creature, and our souls gather neither heat nor life nor light;

[1] Deserved.

for these cannot give to us what they have not in themselves. Oh that we could thrust in through these thorns, and this throng of bastard lovers, and be ravished and sick of love for Christ! We should find some footing and some room, and sweet ease for our tottering and witless souls in our Lord. I wish it were in my power, after this day, to cry down all love but the love of Christ, and to cry down all gods but Christ, all saviours but Christ, all well-beloveds but Christ, and all soul-suitors and love-beggars but Christ.

You complain that you want a mark of the sound work of grace and love in your soul. For answer, consider for your satisfaction (till God send more) 1 *John* 3. 14. And as for your complaint of deadness and doubtings, Christ will, I hope, take your deadness and you together. They are bodies full of holes, running boils, and broken bones which need mending, that Christ the Physician taketh up; whole vessels are not for the Mediator's art. Publicans, sinners, whores, harlots, are ready market-wares for Christ. The only thing that will bring sinners within a cast of Christ's drawing arm is that which you write of – some feeling of death and sin. That bringeth forth complaints; and therefore, out of sense complain more, and be more acquaint with all the cramps, stitches, and soul-swoonings that trouble you. The more pain, and the more night-watching, and the more fevers, the better. A soul bleeding to death till Christ were sent for, and cried for in all haste, to come and stem the blood, and close up the hole in the wound with His own hand and balm, were a very good disease, when many are dying of a whole heart. We have all too little of hell-pain and terrors that way. Nay, God send me such a hell as Christ hath promised to make a heaven of!

Alas! I am not come that far on the way, as to say in sad earnest, 'Lord Jesus, great and sovereign Physician, here is a pained patient for thee'. But the thing that we mistake is the want of victory. We hold that to be the mark of one that hath no grace. Nay, say I, the want of *fighting* were a mark of no grace; but I shall not say the want of *victory* is such a mark. If my fire and the devil's water make crackling like thunder in the air, I am the less feared; for where there is fire, it is Christ's part, which I lay and bind upon him, to keep in the coal, and to pray the Father that my faith fail not, if I in the meantime be wrestling and doing and fighting and mourning. For prayer putteth not Paul's devil (the thorn in the flesh, and the messenger of Satan) to the door at first; but our Lord will have them to try every one, and let Paul fend for himself, by God's help, God keeping the stakes and moderating the play. And you do well not to doubt, if the ground-stone be sure, but to try if it be so; for there is great odds between doubting that we have grace, and trying if we have grace. The former may be sin, but the latter is good.

We are but loose in trying our free-holding of Christ, and making sure work of Christ. Holy fear is a searching of the camp, that there be no enemy within our bosom to betray us, and a seeing that all be fast and sure. For I see many leaky vessels fair before the wind, and professors who take their conversion upon trust, and they go on securely, and see not the under-water, till a storm sink them. Each man had need twice a day, and oftener, to be riped,[1] and searched with candles.

Pray for me, that the Lord would give me house-room again, to hold a candle to this dark world. Grace, grace be with you.

[1] Examined thoroughly, ripped up.

37/TO JOHN HENDERSON [OF RUSCO]

Practical hints

Aberdeen [undated]

Loving Friend:

I earnestly desire your salvation. Know the Lord and seek Christ. You have a soul that cannot die. Seek for a lodging to your poor soul, for that house of clay will fall. Heaven or nothing! either Christ or nothing! Use prayer in your house and set your thoughts often upon death and judgment. It is dangerous to be loose in the matter of your salvation. Few are saved; men go to heaven in ones and twos, and the whole world lieth in sin. Love your enemies and stand by the truth which I have taught you, in all things. Fear not men, but let God be your fear. Your time will not be long; make the seeking of Christ your daily task. Ye may, when ye are in the fields, speak to God. Seek a broken heart for sin, for without that there is no meeting with Christ. I speak this to your wife as well as to yourself. I desire your sister, in her fears and doubtings, to fasten her grips on Christ's love. I forbid her to doubt, for Christ loveth her and hath her name written in his book. Her salvation is fast coming. Christ her Lord is not slow in coming, nor slack in his promise.

Grace be with you.

Your loving pastor,

S.R.

38/TO ALEXANDER COLVILL [OF BLAIR]

Regrets for being silenced in ministry
Longings for Christ

Aberdeen, 23 June 1637

Much honoured Sir:

Grace, mercy and peace be to you. I would desire to know how my lord took my letter I sent him, and how he is. I desire nothing but that he be fast and honest to my royal Master and King. I am well every way, all praise to him, in whose books I must stand for ever as his debtor. Only my silence paineth me. I had one joy out of heaven, next to Christ my Lord, and that was to preach him to this faithless generation; and they have taken that from me. It was to me as the poor man's one eye, and they have put out that eye. I know that the violence done to me and his poor bereft bride is come up before the Lord; and, suppose I see not the other side of my cross, or what my Lord will bring out of it; yet I believe the vision shall not tarry, and that Christ is on his journey for my deliverance. He goeth not slowly, but passeth over ten mountains at one stride.

In the meantime, I am pained with his love, because I want real possession. When Christ cometh, he stayeth not long. But certainly the blowing of his breath upon a poor soul is heaven upon earth; and when the wind turneth into the north, and he goeth away, I die, till the wind change into the west, and he visit his prisoner. But he holdeth me not often at his door. I am richly repaid for suffering for him. O if all Scotland were as I am, except my bonds! O what pain I have, because I cannot get him praised by my sufferings! O that heaven within and without, and the earth, were paper, and all the rivers, fountains, and seas were ink, and I able to write all the paper within and without, full of his praises, and love, and excellency, to be read by man and angel! Nay, this is little; I owe my heaven to Christ, and do desire, although I should never enter in at the gates of the New Jerusalem, to send my love and my praises over the wall to Christ. Alas, that time and days lie betwixt him and me, and adjourn our meeting! It is my part to cry, 'Oh when will the night be past and the day dawn, that we shall see one another!'

Be pleased to remember my service to my lord, to whom I wrote; and show him, that, for his affection to me, I cannot but pray for him, and earnestly desire that Christ miss him not out of the roll of those who are his witnesses, now when his kingly honour is called in question. It is his honour to hold up Christ's royal train, and to be an instrument to hold the crown upon Christ's head. Show him, because I love his true honour and standing, that this is my earnest desire for him. Now I bless you; and the prayers of Christ's prisoner come upon you; and his sweetest presence, whom you serve in the Spirit, accompany you.

39/TO JAMES HAMILTON

Suffering for Christ's Headship
Christ's over-burdened debtor

Aberdeen, 7 July 1637

Reverend and dearly beloved in our Lord:

Grace, mercy and peace be to you. Our acquaintance is neither in bodily presence nor on paper; but as sons of the same Father and sufferers for the same truth.

Let no man doubt that the *state of our question* which we are now forced to stand to by suffering exile and imprisonment is, if Christ should reign over his kirk or not. Oh, if my sinful arm could hold the crown on his head, howbeit it should be stricken off from the shoulder-blade! For your ensuing and feared trial, my very dearest in our Lord Jesus, alas! what am I, to speak comfort to a soldier of Christ who hath done a hundred times more for that worthy and honourable cause than I can do! But I know, those of whom the world was not worthy wandered up and down in deserts and in mountains and in dens and caves of the earth; and while there is one member of mystical Christ out of heaven, that member must suffer strokes, till our Lord Jesus draw in that member within the gates of the New Jerusalem, which he will not fail to do at last; for not one toe or finger of that body, but it shall be taken in within the city. What can be our part in this pitched battle betwixt the Lamb and the Dragon, but to receive the darts in patience that rebound off us upon our sweet Master; or rather, light first upon him, and then rebound off him upon his servants? I think it a sweet north wind, that bloweth first upon the fair face of the Chief among ten thousand, and then lighteth upon our sinful and black faces. When once the wind bloweth off him upon me, I think it hath a sweet smell of Christ; and so must be some more than a single cross. I know that you have a guard about you, and your attendance and train for your safety is far beyond your pursuer's force or fraud. It is good, under feud, to be near our ward-house and stronghold. We can do little to resist them who persecute us and oppose him, but keep our blood and our wounds to the next court-day, when our complaints shall be read. If this day be not Christ's, I am sure the morrow shall be his.

As for anything I do in my bonds, when now and then a word falleth from me, alas! it is very little. I am exceedingly grieved that any should conceive anything to be in such a broken and empty reed. Let no man impute it to me, that the free and unbought wind (for I gave nothing for it) bloweth upon an empty reed. I am his over-burdened debtor. I cry, 'Down with me; down, down with all the excellency of the world; and up, up with Christ!' Long, long may that fair One, that holy One, be on high! My curse be upon them that love him not. O how glad would I be if his glory would grow out and spring up out of my bonds and sufferings! Certainly, since I became his prisoner, he hath won the yolk and heart of my soul. Christ is even become a new Christ to me, and his love greener than it was. And now I strive no more with him; his love shall carry it away. I lay down myself under his love. I desire to sing and to cry and to proclaim myself, even under the water, in his common,[1] and eternally indebted to his kindness. I will not offer to quit commons with him (as we used to say), for that will not be. All, all for evermore to be Christ's! What further trials are before me I know not, but I know that Christ will have a saved soul of me, over on the other side of the water, on the yonderside of crosses, and beyond men's wrongs.

I had but one eye and that they have put out. My one joy, next to the flower of my joys, Christ, was to preach my sweetest, sweetest Master and the glory of his Kingdom; and it seemed no cruelty to them to put out the poor man's one eye. And now I am seeking about to see if *suffering* will speak my fair One's praises, and I am trying if a dumb man's tongue can raise one note, or one of Zion's springs, to advance my Well-beloved's glory. Oh, if he would make some glory to himself out of a dumb prisoner! I go with child of his word; I cannot be delivered. None here will have my Master. Alas! what aileth them at him?

I bless you for your prayers. Add to them praises. As I am able, I pay you home.[2] I commend your diving in Christ's Testament. I would that I could set out the dead man's good-

---

[1] Indebted to, under obligation to.
[2] Reciprocate.

will to his friends in his sweet Testament. Speak a prisoner's hearty commendations to Christ. Fear not, your ten days [*Rev* 2. 10] will over. Those that are gathered against Mount Zion, their eyes shall melt away in their eye-holes, and their tongues consume away in their mouths, and Christ's withered garden shall grow green again in Scotland. My Lord Jesus hath a word hid in heaven for Scotland, not yet brought out.

Grace be with you.

40/TO THE PARISHIONERS OF ANWOTH

Protestation of care for their souls and for the glory of God
Delights in his ministry and in his Lord
Warnings against errors of the day
Words to the backslider
Intense admiration for Christ
A loud call to all

Aberdeen, 13 July 1637

Dearly beloved and longed-for in the Lord, my crown and my joy in the day of Christ:

Grace be to you and peace, from God our Father and from our Lord Jesus Christ.

I long exceedingly to know if the oft-spoken-of match betwixt you and Christ holdeth, and if you follow on to know the Lord. My day-thoughts and my night-thoughts are of you. While you sleep I am afraid of your souls, that they be off the Rock. Next to my Lord Jesus and this fallen kirk, you have the greatest share of my sorrow and also of my joy. You are the matter of tears, care, fear, and daily prayers of an oppressed prisoner of Christ. As I am in bonds for my high and lofty One, my royal and princely Master, my Lord Jesus, so I am in bonds for you. For I should have slept in my warm nest, and kept the fat world in my arms, and the cords of my tabernacle should have been fastened more strongly; I might have sung an evangel of ease to my soul and you for a time, with my brethren, the sons of my mother, that were angry at me and have thrust me out of the vineyard; if I would have been broken, and drawn on to mire you, the Lord's flock, and to cause you to eat pastures trodden upon with men's feet, and to drink foul and muddy waters. But truly the Almighty was a terror to me, and His fear made me afraid. O my Lord, judge if my ministry be not dear to me, but not so dear by many degrees as Christ my Lord!

God knoweth the sad and heavy Sabbaths I have had, since I laid down at my Master's feet my two shepherd's staves. I have been often saying, as it is written, 'My enemies chased me sore like a bird, without cause: they have cut off my life in the dungeon, and cast a stone upon me' (*Lam* 3. 52, 53]. For, next to Christ, I had but one joy, the apple of the eye of my delights, to preach Christ my Lord; and they have violently plucked that away from me. It was to me like the poor man's one eye; and they have put out that eye, and quenched my light in the inheritance of the Lord. But my eye is toward the Lord. I know that I shall see the salvation of God and that my hope shall not always be forgotten. And my sorrow shall want nothing to complete it, and to make me say, 'What availeth it me to live?', if you follow the voice of a stranger, of one that cometh into the sheep-fold, not by Christ the door, but climbeth up another way.

If the man build his hay and stubble upon the golden foundation, Christ Jesus (already laid among you), and you follow him, I assure you, the man's work shall burn and never bide God's fire; and you and he both shall be in danger of everlasting burning except ye repent. Oh, if any pain, any sorrow, any loss that I can suffer for Christ and for you were laid in pledge to buy Christ's love to you! and that I could lay my dearest joys, next to Christ my Lord, in the gap betwixt you and eternal destruction! O if I had paper as broad as heaven and earth, and ink as the sea and all the rivers and fountains of the earth, and were able to write the love, the worth, the excellency, the sweetness and due praises of our dearest and fairest Well-beloved! and then if you could read and understand it! What could I want, if my ministry among you should make a marriage between the little bride in those bounds and the Bridegroom? O how rich a prisoner were I, if I could obtain of my Lord (before whom I stand for you) the salvation of you all! O what a prey had I gotten, to have you catched in Christ's net! O then, I had cast out my Lord's lines and his net with a rich gain! Oh then, well-wared[1] pained breast and sore back and crazed body, in speaking early and late to you!

My witness is above; your heaven would be two heavens to me, and the salvation of you all as two salvations to me. I would subscribe a suspension,[2] and a fristing[3] of my heaven for many hundred years (according to God's good pleasure) if ye were sure in the upper lodging, in our Father's house, before me. I take to witness heaven and earth against you, I take instruments[4] in the hands of that sun and daylight that beheld us, and in the hands of the timber and walls of that kirk, if I drew not up a fair contract of marriage betwixt you and Christ, if I went not with offers betwixt the Bridegroom and you; and your conscience did bear you witness, your mouths confessed, that there were many fair trysts and meetings drawn on betwixt Christ and you at communion feasts and other occasions. There were bracelets, jewels, rings and love-letters sent to you by the Bridegroom. It was told you what a fair dowry you should have, and what a house your Husband and you should dwell in, and what was the Bridegroom's excellency, sweetness, might, power, the eternity and glory of his

[1]See p 101 *fn* 1.
[2]An act in law postponing the carrying out of a decision.   [3]See p 60 *fn* 1.
[4]See p 59 *fn* 2.

kingdom, the exceeding deepness of his love, who sought his black wife through pain, fires, shame, death and the grave, and swimmed the salt sea for her, undergoing the curse of the law, and then[1] was made a curse for you. And you then consented and said, 'Even so I take him'.

I counsel you to beware of the new and strange leaven of men's inventions beside and against the Word of God, contrary to the oath of this Kirk, now coming among you. I instructed you of the superstition and idolatry in kneeling in the instant of receiving the Lord's Supper, and of crossing[2] in baptism, and of the observing of men's days, without any warrant of Christ our perfect Lawgiver. Countenance not the surplice, the attire of the mass-priest, the garment of Baal's priests. The abominable bowing to altars of tree (wood) is coming upon you. Hate and keep yourselves from idols. Forbear in any case to hear the reading of the new fatherless[3] Service-Book,[4] full of gross heresies, popish and superstitious errors, without any warrant of Christ, tending to the overthrow of preaching. You owe no obedience to the bastard canons; they are unlawful, blasphemous, and superstitious. All the ceremonies that lie in Antichrist's foul womb, the wares of that great mother of fornications, the Kirk of Rome, are to be refused. You see whither they lead you. Continue still in the doctrine which you have received. You heard of me the whole counsel of God. Sew no clouts upon Christ's robe. Take Christ, in His rags and losses, and as persecuted by men, and be content to sigh and pant up the mountain, with Christ's cross on your back. Let me be reputed a false prophet (and your conscience once said the contrary) if your Lord Jesus will not stand by you and maintain you, and maintain your cause against your enemies.

I have heard, and my soul is grieved for it, that since my departure from you, many among you are turned back from

---

[1]Thus. [2]Making the sign of the cross.
[3]Without the author's name. [4]See *p* 78 *fn* 1.

the good old way, to the dog's vomit again. Let me speak to these men. It was not without God's special direction that the first sentence that ever my mouth uttered to you was that: 'And Jesus said, For judgment I am come into this world, that they which see not might see; and that they which see might be made blind' [*John* 9. 39]. Is it possible that my first meeting and yours may be when we shall both stand before the dreadful Judge of the world; and in the name and authority of the Son of God, my great King and Master, I write, by these presents, summonses to those men. I arrest their souls and bodies to the day of our compearance.[1] Their eternal damnation standeth subscribed, and sealed in heaven, by the handwriting of the great Judge of quick and dead; and I am ready to stand up, as a preaching witness against such to their face, on that day, and to say 'Amen' to their condemnation, except they repent. The vengeance of the Gospel is heavier than the vengeance of the Law. The Mediator's malediction and vengeance is twice vengeance, and that vengeance is the due portion of such men. And there I leave them as bond men, aye and until they repent and amend.

Ye were witnesses how the Lord's day was spent while I was among you. O sacrilegious robber of God's day, what wilt thou answer the Almighty when he seeketh so many Sabbaths back again from thee? What will the curser, swearer and blasphemer do when his tongue shall be roasted in that broad and burning lake of fire and brimstone? And what will the drunkard do when tongue, lungs and liver, bones and all shall boil and shall fry in a torturing fire? He shall be far from his barrels of strong drink then; and there is not a cold well of water for him in hell. What shall be the case of the wretch, the covetous man, the oppressor, the deceiver, the earth-worm, who can never get his wombful of clay [*Ps* 17. 14], when, in the day of Christ, gold and silver must lie burnt in ashes, and he must compear[1] and answer his Judge, and quit his clayey

[1]See *p* 80 *fn* 1.

R—8

and noughty[1] heaven!

Woe, woe, for evermore, be to the time-turning atheist, who hath one god and one religion for summer, and another god and another religion for winter, and the day of fanning, when Christ fanneth all that is in his barn-floor; who hath a conscience for every fair and market, and the soul of him runneth upon these oiled wheels, time, custom, the world, and command of men. O, if the careless atheist, and sleeping man, who edgeth by all with, 'God forgive our pastors if they lead us wrong, we must do as they command', and layeth down his head upon time's bosom, and giveth his conscience to a deputy, and sleepeth so, till the smoke of hell-fire fly up in his throat, and cause him to start out of his doleful bed! O if such a man would awake! Many woes are for the over-gilded and gold-plastered hypocrite. A heavy doom is for the liar and white-tongued flatterer; and the flying book of God's fearful vengeance, twenty cubits long and ten cubits broad, that goeth out from the face of God, shall enter into the house, and in upon the soul of him that stealeth and sweareth falsely by God's name [*Zech* 5. 2, 3].

I denounce eternal burning, hotter than Sodom's flames, upon the men that boil in filthy lusts of fornication, adultery, incest, and the like wickedness. No room, no, not a foot-breadth, for such vile dogs within the clean Jerusalem. Many of you put off all with this, 'God forgive us, we know no better'. I renew my old answer: the Judge is coming in flaming fire, with all his mighty angels to render vengeance to all those who know not God, and believe not [2 *Thess* 1. 8]. I have often told you that security will slay you. All men say they have faith: as many men and women now, as many saints in heaven. And all believe (say you), so that every foul dog is clean enough, and good enough, for the clean and new Jerusalem above. Every man hath conversion and the new birth; but it is not leal[2] come. They had never a sick night for

[1] Worthless. [2] Honest, genuine.

sin; conversion came to them in a night-dream. In a word, hell will be empty at the day of judgment, and heaven pang[1] full! Alas! it is neither easy nor ordinary to believe and to be saved. Many must stand, in the end, at heaven's gates [*Luke* 13. 25]. When they go to take out their faith, they take out a fair nothing, or (as ye use to speak) a blaflume.[2] O lamentable disappointment! I pray you, I charge you in the name of Christ, make fast work of Christ and salvation.

I know there are some believers among you, and I write to you, O poor broken-hearted believers. All the comforts of Christ in the Old and New Testaments are yours. O what a Father and Husband you have! O, if I had pen and ink, and engine[3] to write of him! Let heaven and earth be consolidated into massy and pure gold, it will not weigh the thousandth part of Christ's love to a soul, even to me a poor prisoner. O that is a massy and marvellous love! Men and angels! unite your force and strength in one, you shall not heave nor poise it off the ground. Ten thousand worlds, as many worlds as angels can number, and then as a new world of angels can multiply, would not all be the balk[4] of a balance to weigh Christ's excellency, sweetness and love. Put ten earths into one, and let a rose grow greater than ten whole earths, or whole worlds, O what beauty would be in it, and what a smell would it cast! But a blast of the breath of that fairest Rose in all God's paradise, even of Christ Jesus our Lord, one look of that fairest face would be infinitely in beauty and smell above all imaginable and created glory!

I wonder that men can bide off[5] Christ. I would esteem myself blessed if I could make an open proclamation, and gather all the world that are living upon the earth, Jew and Gentile, and all that shall be born till the blowing of the last trumpet, to flock round about Christ, and to stand looking, wondering, admiring, and adoring his beauty and sweetness.

[1]Crammed.　[2]A sham, an air-bubble.　[3]See *p* 42 *fn* 1.　[4]Beam.
[5]Abide (stay) away from.

For his fire is hotter than any other fire, his love sweeter than common love, his beauty surpasseth all other beauty. When I am heavy and sad, one of his love-looks would do me meikle worlds' good. O if you would fall in love with him, how blessed were I! How glad would my soul be to help you to love him! But amongst us all, we could not love him enough. He is the Son of the Father's love, and God's delight. The Father's love lieth all upon him. O if all mankind would fetch all their love and lay it upon him! Invite him, and take him home to your houses, in the exercise of prayer morning and evening, as I often desired you; especially now, let him not want lodging in your houses, nor lie in the fields when he is shut out of pulpits and kirks. If you will be content to take heaven by violence and the wind on your face for Christ and his cross, I am here one who hath some trial of Christ's cross, and I can say, that Christ was ever kind to me, but he over-cometh himself (if I may speak so) in kindness while I suffer for him. I give you my word for it, Christ's cross is not so evil as they call it; it is sweet, light, and comfortable. I would not want the visitations of love, and the very breathings of Christ's mouth when he kisseth, and my Lord's delightsome smiles and love-embracements under my sufferings for him, for a mountain of gold, or for all the honours, court, and grandeur of velvet kirkmen. Christ hath the yolk and heart of my love. 'I am my Beloved's and my Well-beloved is mine'.

O that you were hand-fasted to Christ! O my dearly-beloved in the Lord, I would I could change my voice, and had a tongue tuned by the hands of my Lord, and had the art of speaking of Christ, that I might point out to you the worth and highness and greatness and excellency of that fairest and renowned Bridegroom! I beseech you by the mercies of the Lord, by the sighs, tears, and heart's-blood of our Lord Jesus, by the salvation of your poor and precious souls, set up the mountain, that you and I may meet before the Lamb's throne amongst the congregation of the first-born. The Lord grant that that may be the trysting-place! that you and I may put up our hands together, and pluck and eat the apples off the tree of life, and that we may feast together and drink together of that pure river of the water of life that cometh out from the throne of God and of the Lamb!

O how little is your hand-breadth and span-length of days here! Your inch of time is less than when you and I parted. Eternity, eternity is coming, posting on with wings; then shall every man's blacks and whites be brought to light. O how low will your thoughts be of this fair-skinned but heart-rotten apple, the vain, vain, feckless[1] world, when the worms shall make them houses in your eye-holes, and shall eat off the flesh from the balls of your cheeks, and shall make that body a number of dry bones! Think not that the common gate[2] of serving God, as neighbours and others do, will bring you to heaven. Few, few are saved. The devil's court is thick and many. He hath the greatest number of mankind for his vassals. I know this world is a forest of thorns in your way to heaven; but you must go through it. Acquaint yourselves with the Lord; hold fast Christ; hear his voice only. Bless his name; sanctify and keep holy his day; keep the new commandment, 'Love one another'; let the Holy Spirit dwell in your bodies; and be clean and holy.

Love not the world; lie not; love and follow truth. Learn to know God. Keep in mind what I taught you, for God will seek an account of it when I am far from you. Abstain from all evil and all appearance of evil. Follow good carefully, and seek peace and follow after it. Honour your king and pray for him. Remember me to God in your prayers; I cannot forget you.

I told you often while I was with you, and now I write it again; heavy, sad and sore is that stroke of the Lord's wrath that is coming upon Scotland. Woe, woe, woe to this harlot-

[1]See *p* 40 *fn* 1   [2]Way, manner.

land! for they shall take the cup of God's wrath from his hands, and drink and spue and fall and not rise again. In, in, in with speed to your stronghold, you prisoners of hope, and hide you there till the anger of the Lord pass! Follow not the pastors of this land, for the sun is gone down upon them. As the Lord liveth, they lead you from Christ, and from the good old way. Yet the Lord will keep the holy city, and make this withered Kirk to bud again like a rose and a field blessed of the Lord.

The grace of the Lord Jesus Christ be with you all. The prayers and blessings of a prisoner of Christ, in bonds for him, and for you, be with you all. Amen.

Your lawful and loving pastor,

S.R.

41/TO LADY KILCONQUHAR

The interests of the soul most urgent
Folly of the world
Christ altogether lovely
His pen fails to set forth Christ's unspeakable beauty

Aberdeen, 8 August 1637

Mistress:

Grace, mercy and peace be to you. I am glad to hear that you have your face homeward towards your Father's house, now when so many are for a home nearer hand. But your Lord calleth you to another life and glory than is to be found here-away: and therefore I would counsel you to make sure the charters and rights which you have to salvation.

You came to this life about a necessary and weighty business to tryst with Christ concerning your precious soul, the eternal salvation of it. This is the most necessary business you have in this life; and your other concerns beside this are but toys and feathers, and dreams and fancies. This is in the greatest haste, and should be done first. Means are used in the gospel to draw on a meeting betwixt Christ and you. If you neglect your part of it, it is as if you would tear the contract before Christ's eyes, and give up the match, that there may be no more communing about that business. I know that other lovers beside Christ are in suit of you, and your soul hath many wooers. But I pray you make a chaste virgin of your soul, and let it love but one. Most worthy is Christ alone of all your soul's love, even if your love were higher than the heaven, and deeper than the lowest of this earth, and broader than this world. Many, alas, too many, estrange their souls from Christ. Marriage with Christ would put your love and your heart out of the way, and out of the eye of all other unlawful suitors: and then you have a ready answer for all others, 'I am already promised away to Christ, the match is concluded, my soul hath a Husband already, and it cannot have two husbands'.

O that the world did but know what a smell the ointments of Christ cast, and how great his beauty, even the beauty of the fairest of the sons of men, is, and how sweet and powerful his voice is, the voice of that one Well-beloved! Certainly where Christ cometh, he runneth away with the soul's love, so that it cannot be commanded. I would far rather look but through the hole of Christ's door, to see but the one half of his fairest and most comely face (for he looketh like heaven), suppose I should never get in to see his excellency and glory to the full, than to enjoy the flower, the bloom and chief excellency of the glory and riches of ten worlds. Lord send me, for my part, but the meanest share of Christ that can be given to any of the indwellers of the New Jerusalem. But I know my Lord is no niggard: he can, and it becometh him well to give more than my narrow soul can receive. If there were ten thousand thousand millions of worlds, and as many heavens full of men and angels, Christ would not be pinched to supply all our wants, and to fill us all. Christ is a well of life, but who knoweth how deep it is to the bottom?

This soul of ours hath love, and cannot but love some fair one; and O what a fair One, what an only One, what an excellent, lovely One is Jesus! Put the beauty of ten thousand thousand worlds of paradises like the garden of Eden in one; put all trees, all flowers, all smells, all colours, all tastes, all joys, all sweetness, all loveliness in one. O what a fair and excellent thing would that be! And yet it would be less, to that fair and dearest Well-beloved, Christ, than one drop of rain to the whole seas, rivers, lakes and fountains of ten thousand earths. O, but Christ is heaven's wonder, and earth's wonder! What marvel that his bride saith, 'He is altogether lovely!' [*Cant* 5. 16]. Alas that black souls will not come, and fetch all their love to this fair One!

O if I could invite and persuade thousands, and ten thousand times ten thousand of Adam's sons, to flock about my Lord Jesus, and to come and take their fill of love! O pity for evermore that there should be such an one as Christ Jesus, so boundless, so bottomless, and so incomparable in infinite excellency and sweetness, and so few to take him! Oh! oh! you poor, dry and dead souls, why will you not come hither with your empty souls to this huge, and fair, and deep, and sweet well of life; and fill all your empty vessels. O that Christ should be so large in sweetness and worth, and we so narrow, so pinched, so ebb, and so void of all happiness! and yet men will not take him! They lose their love miserably who will not bestow it upon this lovely One.

Alas! these five thousand years Adam's fools have been wasting and lavishing out their love and their affections upon black lovers, upon bits of dead creatures, and broken idols, upon this and that feckless[1] creature; and have not brought their love and their heart to Jesus. O pity, that Fairness hath so few lovers! O, woe, woe to the fools of this world, who

[1] See p 40 *fn* 1.

run by Christ to other lovers! O misery, misery, misery, that Comeliness can scarce get three or four hearts in a town or country! O, that there is so much spoken, and so much written, and so much thought of creature-vanity, and so little spoken, so little written, and so little thought of my great and incomprehensible, and never-enough wondered at Lord Jesus! Why should I not curse this forlorn and wretched world, that suffereth my Lord Jesus to lie alone? O damned souls! O mistaken world! O blind, O beggarly and poor souls! O bewitched fools! what aileth you that you run so from Christ? I dare not challenge Providence, that there are so few buyers and so little sale for such an excellent one as Christ. O the depth, and O the height of my Lord's ways, that pass finding out! But O that men would once be wise, and not fall so in love with their own hell as to pass by Christ, and misken[1] him!

But let us come near and fill ourselves with Christ, and let his friends drink and satisfy our hollow and deep desires with Jesus. O come all and drink at this living well; come, drink and live for evermore, come, drink and welcome. 'Welcome,' saith our fairest Bridegroom. No man getteth Christ with ill-will; no man cometh and is not welcome; no man cometh and rueth his voyage; all men speak well of Christ who have been with him. Men and angels who know him will say more than I can do, and think more of him than they can say. O that I were misted and bewildered in my Lord's love![2] O that I were fettered and chained to it! O sweet pain, to be pained for a sight of him! O living death! O good death! O lovely death, to die for love of Jesus! O that I should have a sore heart and a pained soul for the want of this and that idol! Woe, woe to the mistakings of my miscarrying heart, that gapeth and crieth for creatures, and is not pained, and tortured, and in sorrow for the want of a soul's-fill of the love of Christ!

[1]See *p* 54 *fn* 2.   [2]That is, lost in his love.

O that thou wouldst come near, my Beloved! O my fairest One, why standest thou afar? Come hither, that I may be satiated with thy excellent love. O for a union! O for a fellowship with Jesus! O that I could buy with a price that lovely One, even suppose that hell's torments for a while were the price! I cannot believe but that Christ will take pity upon his pained lovers, and come and ease sick hearts, who sigh and swoon for want of Christ.

What heaven can there be liker to hell than to desire and dwine,[1] and fall a-swoon for Christ's love, and to want it? is not this hell and heaven woven through each other? Is not this pain and joy, sweetness and sadness in one web, the one the weft, the other the warp! Therefore I would that Christ would let us meet, and join together, the soul and Christ in other's arms. O what meeting is like this, to see blackness and beauty, contemptibleness and glory, highness, and baseness, even a soul and Christ, kiss each other! Nay, but when all is done, I may be wearied in speaking and writing; but O how far am I from the right expression of Christ or his love! I can neither speak, nor write feeling, nor tasting, nor smelling; come feel, and smell, and taste Christ and his love, and you shall call it more than can be spoken; to write how sweet the honey-comb is, is not so lovely as to eat and suck the honey-comb. Rest, with Christ, will say more than heart can think or tongue can utter.

Neither need we fear crosses, or sigh or be sad for any thing that is on this side of heaven, if we have Christ. Our crosses will never draw blood of the joy of the Holy Ghost and peace of conscience. Our joy is laid up in such a high place that temptations cannot climb up to take it down. This world may boast against Christ, but they dare not strike; or if they strike, they break their arm in fetching a stroke upon a Rock.

O that we could put our treasure in Christ's hand, and give him our gold to keep, and our crown. Strive, mistress, to

[1] Pine away for.

thring[1] through the thorns of this life to be with Christ; tine[2] not sight of him in this cloudy and dark day; sleep with him in your heart in the night. Learn not from the world to serve Christ, but speer at[3] himself the way; the world is a false copy, and a lying guide to follow.

42/TO LORD CRAIGHALL

Standing for Christ
Danger from fear and the falsity of men
Christ's requitals for suffering
Sin against the Holy Ghost

Aberdeen, 10 August 1637

My Lord:

I received one letter of your Lordship's from C. and another of late from A.B., wherein I find your Lordship is in perplexity what to do. But let me entreat your Lordship not to cause yourself to mistake truth and Christ, because they seem to encounter with[4] your peace and ease. My Lord, remember, that a prisoner hath written it to you, 'As the Lord liveth, if you put to your hand with other apostates in this land, to pull down the sometime beautiful tabernacle of Christ in this land, and join hands with them in one hairbreadth, to welcome Antichrist to Scotland, there is wrath gone out from the Lord against you and your house'. If the terror of a king hath overtaken you, and your Lordship looketh to sleep in your nest in peace, and to take the nearest shore, there are many ways (too, too many ways) how to shift Christ with some ill-washen and foul distinctions. But assure yourself, suppose a king should assure you he would be your god (as he shall never be) for that

[1] To push in by force. [2] Lose. [3] Ask of. [4] Oppose.

piece of service, your clay-god shall die; and your carnal counsellors, when your conscience shall storm against you, and you complain to them, will say, 'What is that to us?' Believe not that Christ is weak, or that he is not able to save. Of two fires that you cannot pass, take the least.

Some few years will bring us all out in our blacks and whites before our Judge. Eternity is nearer to you than you are aware of. To go on in a course of defection, when an enlightened conscience is stirring, and looking you in the face, and crying within you that you are going in an evil way, is a step to the sin against the Holy Ghost. Either many of this land are near that sin, or else I know not what it is. And if this, for which I now suffer, be not the way of peace, and the King's highway to salvation, I believe there is not a way at all. There is not such breadth and elbow-room in the way to heaven as men believe.

Howbeit this day be not Christ's, the morrow shall be his. I believe assuredly that our Lord shall repair the old waste places, and his ruined houses in Scotland; and this wilderness shall yet blossom as the rose. My very worthy and dear Lord, wait upon him, 'who hideth his face from the house of Jacob', and look for him; wait patiently a little upon the Bridegroom's return, that your soul may live, and that you may rejoice with the Lord's inheritance. I dare pledge my life for it, if you take this storm with borne-down Christ, your sky shall quickly clear, and your fair morning dawn. Think (as the truth is) that Christ is just now saying, 'And will you also leave me?' You have a fair occasion to gratify Christ now, if you will stay with him, and want the night's sleep with your suffering Saviour one hour, now when Scotland hath fallen asleep and leaveth Christ to shift for himself.

I profess myself but a weak, feeble man. When I came first to Christ's camp I had nothing to maintain this war, or to bear me out in this encounter, and I am little better yet. But since I find furniture, armour and strength from the consecrated

Captain, the Prince of our salvation, who was perfected through suffering, I esteem suffering for Christ a king's life. I find that our wants qualify us for Christ. And howbeit your Lordship writes that you despair to attain to such a communion and fellowship (which I would not have you to think), yet, would you nobly and courageously venture to make over to Christ, for his honour now lying at the stake, your estate, place and honour, he would lovingly and largely requite you and give you a King's word for a recompense. Venture upon Christ's '*Come*', and I dare affirm you shall say, as it is, 'I bless the Lord who gave me counsel.' [*Ps* 16. 7].

My very worthy Lord, many eyes in both the kingdoms are upon you now, and the eye of our Lord is upon you. Acquit yourself manfully for Christ. Spoil not this good play. Subscribe a blank submission, and put it in Christ's hands. Win, win the blessings and prayers of your sighing and sorrowful mother-church, seeking your help. Win Christ's bond (who is a King of his word) for a hundred-fold more even in this life. If a weak man hath passed a promise to a king to make slip to Christ,[1] (if we look to flesh and blood, I wonder not of it; possibly I might have done worse myself), add not further guiltiness, to go on in such a scandalous and foul way. Remember that there is a woe: 'Woe to him by whom offences come'. This woe came out of Christ's mouth, and it is heavier than the woe of the law. It is the Mediator's vengeance, and that is two vengeances to those who are enlightened.

Free yourself from unlawful anguish about advising, and resolving. When the truth is come to your hand, hold it fast, go not again to make a new search and inquiry for truth. It is easy to make conscience believe as you will, not as you know. It is easy for you to cast your light into prison, and detain God's truth in unrighteousness; but that prisoner will break

[1] That is, if you, in a moment of weakness, have made a rash promise that runs contrary to Christ's interests.

ward to your incomparable torture. Fear your light, and stand in awe of it; for it is from God. Think what honour it is in this life also to be enrolled to the succeeding ages among Christ's witnesses, standing against the re-entry of Antichrist. I know certainly, that your light, looking in two ways and to the two sides, crieth shame upon the course that they would counsel you to follow. The way that is co-partner with the smoke of this fat world [Ps 37. 20], and with wit and ease, smelleth strong of a foul and false way. The Prince of peace, he who brought again from the dead the great Shepherd of his sheep, by the blood of the eternal covenant, establish you, and give you sound light, and counsel you to follow Christ. Grace be with you.

43/TO HUGH M'KAIL

> *The Law*
> *This world is under Christ's control*
> *The security of believers*

Aberdeen, 5 September 1637

My very dear Brother:

Ye know that men may take their sweet fill of the sour Law, in grace's ground, and betwixt the Mediator's breasts. And this is the sinner's safest way; for there is a bed for wearied sinners to rest them in, in the New Covenant, though no bed of Christ's making to sleep in. The Law shall never be my doomster,[1] by Christ's grace. If I get no more good of it (I shall find a sore enough doom in the Gospel to humble and to cast me down), it is, I grant, a good rough friend to follow

---

[1]Pronouncer of sentence.

a traitor to the bar, and to back him till he come to Christ. We may blame ourselves, who cause the Law to crave well-paid debt, to scare us away from Jesus, and dispute about a righteousness of our own, a world in the moon, a chimera, and a night-dream that pride is father and mother to. There cannot be a more humble soul than a believer; it is no pride for a drowning man to catch hold of a rock.

I rejoice that the wheels of this confused world are rolled and cogged and driven according as our Lord willeth. Out of whatever airth[1] the wind blow, it will blow us on our Lord. No wind can blow our sails overboard, because Christ's skill and the honour of his wisdom are empawned[2] and laid down at the stake for the sea-passengers, that he shall put them safe off his hand on the shore, in his Father's known bounds, our native home ground.

My dear brother, scaur[3] not at the cross of Christ. It is not seen yet what Christ will do for you when it cometh to the worst. He will keep his grace till you be at a strait, and then bring forth the decreed birth for your salvation [*Zeph* 2. 2]. You are an arrow of his own making. Let him shoot you against a wall of brass, your point shall keep whole. I cannot, for multitude of letters and distraction of friends, prepare what I would for the times. I have not one hour of spare time, suppose the day were forty hours long.

Remember me in prayer. Grace be with you.

[1]See p 73 *fn* 2.   [2]Laid down as pledge.
[3]Take fright.

44/TO FULK ELLIS

Friends in Ireland
Difficulties in providence
Sinning against light
Constant need of Christ

Aberdeen, 7 September 1637

Worthy and much honoured in our Lord:

Grace, mercy and peace be to you. I am glad of our more than paper-acquaintance. Seeing we have one Father, it reckoneth the less though we never saw one another's face. I profess myself most unworthy to follow the camp of such a worthy and renowned Captain as Christ. Alas! I have cause to be grieved, that men expect anything of such a wretched man as I am. It is a wonder to me, if Christ can make any thing of my naughty, short, and narrow love to him: surely it is not worth the uptaking.

As for our lovely and beloved church in Ireland, my heart bleedeth for her desolation; but I believe our Lord is only lopping the vine-trees, but not intending to cut them down or root them out. It is true (seeing we are heart-atheists by nature, and cannot take Providence aright, because we halt and crook ever since we fell), we dream of a halting Providence, as if God's yard whereby he measureth joy and sorrow to the sons of men were crooked and unjust because servants ride on horseback, and princes go on foot. But our Lord dealeth good and evil, and some one portion or other to both, by ounce-weights; and measureth them in a just and even balance. It is but folly to measure the Gospel by summer or winter weather. The summer sun of the saints shineth not on them in this life. How should we have complained, if the Lord had turned the same Providence, that we now stomach at, up-side down, and had ordered matters thus, that first the saints should have enjoyed heaven, glory, and ease, and then Methuselah's days of sorrow and daily miseries! We would think a short heaven no heaven; certainly his ways pass finding out.

You complain of the evil of heart-atheism; but it is to a greater atheist than any man can be, that you write of that. Oh, light findeth not that reverence and fear which a plant of God's setting should find in our soul! How do we by nature, as others, detain and 'hold captive the truth of God in unrighteousness', and so make God's light a bound prisoner! And even when the prisoner breaketh the jail, and cometh out in belief of a Godhead, and in some practice of holy obedience, how often do we again lay hands on the prisoner, and put our light again in fetters! Certainly there cometh great mist and clouds from the lower part of our soul, our earthly affections, to the higher part which is our conscience, either natural or renewed; as smoke in a lower house breaketh up, and defileth the house above. If we had more practice of obedience, we should have more sound light. I think, lay aside all other guiltiness, that this one, the violence done to God's candle in our soul, were a sufficient dittay[1] against us. There is no helping of this, but by striving to stand in awe of God's light, lest light tell tales of us we desire but little to hear. But since it is not without God that light sitteth neighbour to will, a lawless lord, no marvel that such a neighbour should leaven our judgment and darken our light. I see there is a necessity that we protest against the doings of the old man, and raise up a party against our worst half, to accuse, condemn, sentence, and with sorrow bemoan the dominion of sin's kingdom; and withal, make law, in the new covenant, against our guiltiness; for Christ once condemned sin in the flesh, and we are to condemn it over again.

And if there had not been such a thing as the grace of Jesus,

[1] Indictment.

I should have long since given up with heaven, and with the expectation to see God. But grace, grace, free grace, the merits of Christ for nothing, white and fair, and large Saviour-mercy (which is another sort of thing than creature-mercy, or law-mercy, yea, a thousand degrees above angel-mercy) hath been and must be the rock that we drowned souls must swim to. New washing, renewed application of purchased redemption by that sacred blood that sealeth the free covenant, is a thing of daily and hourly use to a poor sinner. Till we be in heaven, our issue of blood will not be quite dried up; and therefore we must resolve to apply peace to our souls from the new and living Way; and Jesus, who cleanseth and cureth the leprous soul, lovely Jesus, must be our song on this side of heaven's gates. And even when we have won the castle, then must we eternally sing, 'Worthy, worthy is the Lamb, who hath saved us, and washed us in his own blood'.

I would counsel all the ransomed ones to learn this song, and to drink and be drunk with the love of Jesus. O fairest, O highest, O loveliest One, open the well! O water the burnt and withered travellers with this love of thine! I think it is possible on earth to build a young New Jerusalem, a little new heaven, of this surpassing love. God either send me more of this love, or take me quickly over the water, where I may be filled with his love. My softness cannot take with want; I profess I bear not hunger of Christ's love fair; I know not if I play foul play with Christ, but I would have a link of that chain of his Providence mended, in pining and delaying the hungry onwaiters. For myself, I could wish that Christ would let out upon me more of that love. Yet to say Christ is a niggard to me, I dare not; and if I say I have abundance of his love, I should lie: I am half-straitened to complain and cry, Lord Jesus, hold thy hand no longer.

Worthy sir, let me have your prayers in my bonds. Grace be with you.

45/TO JAMES LINDSAY

Desertions and their use
Prayers of reprobates
How the Gospel affects the responsibility of reprobates

Aberdeen, 7 September 1637

Dear Brother:

The constant and daily observing of God's going along with you in his coming, going, ebbing, flowing, embracing, and kissing, glooming and striking, giveth me, a witless and lazy observer of the Lord's way and working, a heavy stroke. Could I keep sight of Him, and know when I want, and behave as became me in that condition, I would bless my case.

Anent desertions, I think them like lean and weak land lying fallow, for some years, while it gathers sap for a better crop. It is possible to gather gold, where it may be had, by moon-light. O if I could but creep one foot, or half a foot, nearer into Jesus, in such a dismal night as that when he is away, I should think it a happy absence!

If I knew the Beloved were only gone away for trial, and for further humiliation, and not smoked out of the house with new provocations, I would forgive desertions, and hold my peace at his absence; but Christ's bought absence (bought with my sin) is two running boils at once, one upon either side; and what side then can I lie on?

I know that, as night and shadows are good for flowers, and moon-light and dews are better than a continual sun, so is Christ's absence of special use, and it hath some nourishing virtue in it, and giveth sap to humility, and putteth an edge on hunger, and furnisheth a fair field to faith to put forth itself, and to exercise its fingers in gripping it seeth not what.

It is mercy's wonder, and grace's wonder, that Christ will

lend a piece of the lodging, and a back-chamber beside himself, to our lusts, and that he and such swine should keep house together in our soul. For suppose they couch and contract themselves into little room when Christ cometh in, and seem to lie as dead under his feet, yet they often break out again: and a foot of the old man, or a leg or arm nailed to Christ's cross looseth the nail, or breaketh out again! And yet Christ, beside this unruly and misnurtured neighbour, can still be making heaven in the saints, one way or other. May not I say, 'Lord Jesus, what doest thou here?' Yet here he must be. But I will not lose my feet to go on into this depth and wonder; for free mercy and infinite merits took a lodging to Christ and us, beside such a loathsome guest as sin.

Sanctification and mortification of our lusts are the hardest part of Christianity. It is in a manner as natural to us to leap when we see the New Jerusalem as to laugh when we are tickled. Joy is not under command, or at our nod, when Christ kisseth. But oh! how many of us would have Christ divided into two halves, that we might take the half of him only! We take his office, Jesus and salvation: but 'Lord' is a cumbersome word; and to obey, and work out our own salvation, and to perfect holiness, is the cumbersome and stormy northside of Christ; and that we eschew and shift.

For your question, the access that reprobates have to Christ (which is none at all: for to the Father in Christ neither can they nor will they come, because Christ died not for them; and yet, by law, God and justice overtaketh them): I say, first, there are with you more worthy and learned than I am – Messrs Dickson, Blair, and Hamilton, who can more fully satisfy you. But I shall speak in brief what I think of it, in these assertions:

First assertion: All God's justice toward man and angels floweth from an act of the absolute, sovereign free-will of God, who is our Former and Potter, and we are but clay; for if he had forbidden to eat of the rest of the trees of the garden of Eden, and commanded Adam to eat of the tree of knowledge of good and evil, that command no doubt had been as just as this, 'Eat of all the trees, but not at all of the tree of knowledge of good and evil'. The reason is, because his will is before his justice, by order of nature; and what is his will is his justice; and he willeth not things without himself because they are just. God cannot, God needeth not hunt sanctity, holiness, or righteousness from things without himself, and so not from the actions of men or angels; because his will is essentially holy and just, and the prime rule of holiness and justice, as the fire is naturally light, and inclineth upwards, and the earth heavy, and inclineth downward.

The *second* assertion then, that God saith to reprobates, 'Believe in Christ (who hath not died for your salvation) and ye shall be saved', is just and right; because his eternal and essentially just will hath so enacted and decreed. Suppose natural reason speak against it, this is the deep and special mystery of the gospel. God hath obliged, hard and fast, all the reprobates of the visible church to believe this promise, 'He that believeth shall be saved'; and yet, in God's decree and secret intention, there is no salvation at all decreed and intended to reprobates. And yet the obligation of God, being from his sovereign free-will, is most just, as is said in the first assertion.

Third assertion: The righteous Lord hath right over the reprobates and all reasonable creatures that violate his commandments. This is easy.

Fourth assertion: The faith that God seeketh of reprobates is, that they rely upon Christ, as despairing of their own righteousness, leaning wholly and withal humbly, as weary and laden, upon Christ, as on the resting-stone laid in Zion. But he seeketh not that, without being weary of their sin, they rely on Christ as mankind's Saviour; for to rely on Christ, and not to be weary of sin, is presumption, not faith. Faith is ever neighbour to a broken and contrite spirit; and it is impossible that faith can be where there is not a cast-down and contrite heart, in some measure, for sin. Now it is certain that God commandeth no man to presume.

Fifth assertion: Then reprobates are not absolutely obliged to believe that Christ died for them in particular. For in truth, neither reprobates nor others are obliged to believe a lie; only they are obliged to believe that Christ died for them, if they be first weary, burdened, sick and condemned in their own consciences, and stricken dead and killed with the law's sentence, and have indeed embraced him as offered; which is a second and subsequent act of faith, following after a coming to him and a closing with him.

Sixth assertion: Reprobates are not formally guilty of contempt of God, and misbelief, because they apply not Christ and the promises of the gospel to themselves in particular; for so they should be guilty because they believe not a lie, which God never obliged them to believe.

Seventh assertion: Justice hath a right to punish reprobates, because from pride of heart, confiding in their own righteousness, they rely not upon Christ as a Saviour of all them that come to him. This God may justly oblige them unto, because in Adam they had perfect ability to do; and men are guilty because thay love their own inability, and rest upon themselves, and refuse to deny their own righteousness, and to take themselves to Christ, in whom there is righteousness for wearied sinners.

Eighth assertion: It is one thing to rely, lean, and rest upon Christ, in humility and weariness of spirit, denying our own righteousness, believing him to be the only righteousness of wearied sinners; and it is another thing to believe that Christ died for me, John, Thomas, Anna, upon an intention and decree to save us by name. For

1. The former goeth first, the latter is always after in due order.
2. The first is faith, the second is a fruit of faith; and

3. The first obligeth reprobates and all men in the visible kirk, the latter obligeth only the weary and laden, and so only the elect and effectually called of God.

Ninth assertion: It is a vain conclusion, 'I know not whether Christ died for me, John, Thomas, Anna, by name; and therefore I dare not rely on him'. The reason is, because it is not faith to believe God's intention and decree of election at the first, ere you be wearied. Look first to your own intention and soul, and if you find sin a burden, and can and do rest under that burden upon Christ; if this be once, now come and believe *in particular*, or rather *apply by sense and feeling* (for in my judgment it is a *fruit* of belief, not belief) the good will, intention, and gracious purpose of God concerning your salvation. Hence, because there is malice in reprobates, and contempt of Christ, guilty they are, and justice hath law against them: and (which is the mystery) they cannot come up to Christ, because he died not for them; but their sin is that they love their inability to come to Christ; and he who loveth his chains deserveth chains.

And thus in short. Remember my bonds.

46/TO JAMES HAMILTON

Christ's glory not affected by his people's weakness
Aberdeen, 7 September 1637

Reverend and dear Brother:

Peace be to you from God our Father and from our Lord Jesus. I am laid low, when I remember what I am, and that my outside casteth such a lustre, when I find so little within. It is a wonder that Christ's glory is not defiled, running through such an unclean and impure channel. But I see that Christ will be Christ, in the dreg and refuse of men. His art, his shining wisdom, his beauty speak loudest in blackness, weakness, deadness, yea, in nothing. I see nothing, no money, no worth, no good, no life, no deserving, is the ground that Omnipotency delighteth to draw glory out of. O how sweet is the inner side of the walls of Christ's house, and a room beside himself! My distance from him maketh me sad. O that we were in each other's arms! O that the middle things betwixt us were removed! I find it a difficult matter to keep all stots[1] with Christ. When he laugheth, I scarce believe it, I would so fain have it true. But I am like a low man looking up to a high mountain, whom weariness and fainting overcometh. I would climb up, but I find that I do not advance in my journey as I would wish. Yet I trust that he will take me home against night. I marvel not that Antichrist, in his slaves, is so busy; but our crowned King seeth and beholdeth, and will arise for Zion's safety.

I am exceedingly distracted with letters and company that visit me. What I can do, or time will permit, I shall not omit. Excuse my brevity, for I am straitened. Remember the Lord's prisoner, I desire to be mindful of you. Grace, grace be with you.

[1] Keep pace.

47/TO LADY GAITGIRTH

> *Christ an example in cross-bearing*
> *The extent to which children should be loved*
> *Why saints die*

Aberdeen, 7 September 1637

Much honoured and Christian Lady:

Grace, mercy and peace be to you. I long to hear how it goeth with you and your children. I exhort you not to lose breath, nor to faint in your journey. The way is not so long to your home as it was; it will wear to one step or an inch at length, and you shall come ere long to be within your arm-length of the glorious crown. Your Lord Jesus did sweat and pant ere he got up that mount. He was at, 'Father, save me', with it. It was he who said, 'I am poured out like water: all my bones are out of joint [Christ was as if they had broken him upon the wheel]: my heart is like wax; it is melted in the midst of my bowels' [Ps 22. 14]. 'My strength is dried up like a potsherd' [verse 15]. I am sure you love the way the better because his holy feet trod it before you. Our crosses have a smell of the crosses and pains of Christ. I believe that your Lord will not leave you to die alone in the way.

I know that you have sad hours when the Comforter is hid under a vail, and when you inquire for him, and find but a toom[1] nest. This, I grant, is but a cold 'good-day' when the seeker misseth him whom the soul loveth. But even his unkindness is kind, his absence lovely, his mask a sweet sight, till God send Christ himself in his own sweet presence. Make his sweet comforts your own, and be not strange and shame-faced with Christ. Homely dealing is best for him; it is his liking. When your winter-storms are over, the summer of your Lord

[1] Empty.

shall come; your sadness will turn to joy, he will do you good in the latter end.

Take no heavier list[1] of your children than your Lord alloweth. Give them room beside your heart, but not in the yolk of your heart, where Christ should be; for then they are your idols, not your bairns. If your Lord take any of them home to his house before the storm come on, take it well. The owner of the orchard may take down two or three apples off his own trees before midsummer, and ere they get the harvest sun; and it would not be seemly that his servant, the gardener, should chide him for it. Let our Lord pluck his own fruit at any season he pleaseth. They are not lost to you, but are laid up so well as that they are offered in heaven, where our Lord's best jewels lie. They are all free goods that are there; death can have no law to arrest any thing that is within the walls of the New Jerusalem.

All the saints, because of sin, are like old rusty horologues,[2] that must be taken down, and the wheels scoured and mended, and set up again in better case than before. Sin hath rusted both soul and body. Our dear Lord by death taketh us down to scour the wheels of both, and to purge us perfectly from the root and remainder of sin. And we shall be set up in better case than before. Then pluck up your heart; heaven is yours; and that is a word few can say. Now the great Shepherd of the sheep, and the very God of peace, confirm and establish you, to the day of the appearance of Christ our Lord.

[1] Joy, delight.   [2] Clocks.

48/TO MARION M'NAUGHT

Prospects of his ministry
Hopes
Salutations

Aberdeen, 7 September 1637

Much honoured and dearest in our sweet Lord Jesus:

Grace, mercy and peace from God our Father and from our Lord Jesus.

I know that the Lord will do for your town. I hear that the Bishop is afraid to come amongst you: for so it is spoken in this town. And many here rejoice now to pen a supplication to the Council, for bringing me home to my place, and for repairing other wrongs done in the country: and see if you can procure that three or four hundred in the country, noblemen, gentlemen, countrymen and citizens, subscribe it; the more the better. It may be that it will affright the Bishop; and, by law, no advantage can be taken against you for it. I have not time to write to Carleton and to Knockbrex, but I would you did speak them in it, and let them advise with Carleton. Mr A. thinketh well of it, and I think the others will approve it.

I am still in good case with Christ; my court is no less than it was; the door of the Bridegroom's house of wine is open, when such a poor stranger as I come athwart. I change, but Christ abideth still the same.

They have put out my one poor eye, my only joy, to preach Christ and to go errands betwixt him and his bride. What my Lord will do with me I know not: it is like that I shall not winter in Aberdeen, but where it shall be else I know not. There are some blossomings of Christ's kingdom in this town, and the smoke is rising, and the ministers are raging; but I love a rumbling and roaring devil best.

I beseech you in the Lord, my dear sister, to wait for the salvation of God. Slack not your hands in meeting to pray. Fear not flesh and blood: we have been over-feared, and that gave louns[1] the confidence to shut me out of Galloway.

Remember my love to John Carsen and Mr John Brown. I never could get my love off that man: I think Christ hath something to do with him. Desire your husband from me not to think ill of Christ for his cross. Many misken Christ because he hath the cross on his back, but he will cause us all to laugh yet. I beseech you, as you would do anything for me, to remember my Lady Marischal[2] to God, and her son the Earl Marischal, especially her Christian daughter, my Lady Pitsligo.

I shall go to death with it, that Christ will return again to Scotland with salvation in his wings, and to Galloway.

Grace be with you.

49/TO JAMES BAUTIE

Spiritual difficulties resolved

Aberdeen, 1637

Loving Brother:

Grace, mercy and peace be unto you. I received your letter, and render you thanks for the same; but I have not time to answer all the heads of it, as the bearer can inform you.

1. You do well to take yourself at the right stot,[3] when you wrong Christ by doubting and misbelief; for this is to nick-name Christ, and term him a liar, which, being spoken to our Prince, would be hanging or beheading. But

---

[1] Rogues.   [2] She was widowed in October 1635.
[3] The rebound of a ball (that is, recall your thoughts before they have gone too far).

Christ hangeth not always for treason. It is good that he may registrate[1] a believer's bond a hundred times, and more than seven times a day have law against us, and yet He spareth us, as a man doth his son that serveth him. No tender-hearted mother, who may have law to kill her sucking-child, would put in execution that law.

2. For your failings, even when you have a set tryst with Christ, and when you have a fair, seen advantage, by keeping your appointment with him, and salvation cometh to the very passing of the seals, I would say two things. (1) Concluded and sealed salvation may go through and be ended, suppose you write your name to the covenant with ink that can hardly be read. Neither think I any man's salvation ever passed the seals, but there was an odd trick or slip, less or more, upon the fool's part, who is enfeoffed[2] in heaven. In the most grave and serious work of our salvation, I think Christ had ever good cause to laugh at our silliness, and to put on us his merits, that we might bear weight. (2) It is a sweet law of the new covenant, and a privilege of the new burgh, that citizens pay according to their means; for the new covenant saith not, 'So much obedience by ounce-weights, and no less, under the pain of damnation'. Christ taketh as poor men may give. Where there is a mean portion, he is content with the less, if there be sincerity. Broken sums and little weak obedience will be pardoned, and hold their footing with him. Know you not that our kindly Lord retaineth his good old heart yet? 'He breaketh not a bruised reed, nor quencheth the smoking flax'; if the wind but blow, he holdeth his hands about it till it rise to a flame. The law cometh on with three O-yeses – 'with all the heart, with all the soul, and with all the whole strength'; and where would poor folks, like you and me, furnish all these sums? It feareth me, nay, it is most

---

[1] Register, keep on record.
[2] Invested with a right to heaven.

certain, that if the payment were to come out of our purse, when we should put our hand into our bag, we should bring out the wind, or worse. But the new covenant seeketh not heap-mete,[1] nor stented[2] obedience, as the condition of it, because forgiveness hath always place. Hence I draw this conclusion: that to think matters betwixt Christ and us go back for want of heaped measure, is a piece of old Adam's pride, who would either be at legal payment or nothing. We would still have God in our common, and buy his kindness with our merits. For beggarly pride is devil's honesty, and blusheth to be in Christ's common,[3] and scarce giveth God a gramercy,[4] and a lifted cap (except it be the Pharisee's 'God I thank thee'), or a bowed knee to Christ. It will only give a 'Goodday' for a 'Good-day' again; and if he dissemble his kindness, as it were, and seem to misken it, it in earnest spurneth with the heels, and snuffeth in the wind, and careth not much for Christ's kindness. 'If he will not be friends, let him go', saith pride. Beware of this thief, when Christ offereth himself.

3. No marvel then of whisperings, whether you be in the covenant or not? for pride maketh loose work of the covenant of grace, and will not let Christ be full bargainmaker. To speak to you particularly and shortly. (1) All the truly regenerated cannot determinately tell you the measure of their dejections; because Christ beginneth young with many, and stealeth into their heart ere they are aware, and becometh homely with them, with little din or noise. I grant that many are blinded, in rejoicing in a good-cheap[5] conversion, that never cost them a sick night; Christ's physic wrought in a dream upon them. But for that, I would say, if other marks be found that Christ is indeed come in, never make plea with him, because he will

---

[1]Full (heaped) measure. [2]Fixed at a certain rate. [3]To be indebted to Christ (Cf p 108 fn 1.) [4]Thank-you. [5]Gratuitous.

not answer, 'Lord Jesus, how camest thou in? whether in at door or window?' Make him welcome since he is come. 'The wind bloweth where it listeth.' All the world's wit cannot perfectly render a reason why the winds should be a month in the east, six weeks possibly in the west, and the space only of an afternoon in the south or north. You will not find out all the steps of Christ's way with a soul, do what you can; for sometimes he will come in stepping softly, like one walking beside a sleeping person, and slip to the door, and let none know he was there. (2) You object that the truly regenerate should love God for himself: and you fear that you love him more for his benefits, as incitements and motives to love him, than for himself. I answer: to love God for himself as the last end, and also for his benefits, as incitements and motives to love him, may stand well together; as a son loveth his mother, because she is his mother, howbeit she be poor; and he loveth her for an apple also. I hope that you will not say that benefits are the only reason and bottom of your love; it seemeth there is a better foundation for it. Always, if a hole be in it, sew it up shortly.[1] (3) You feel not such mourning in Christ's absence as you would. I answer: That the regenerate mourn at all times, and all in a like measure, for his absence, I deny. There are different degrees of mourning, less or more, as they have less or more love to him, and less or more sense of his absence; but, some they must have. Sometimes they miss not the Lord, and then they cannot mourn; howbeit it is not long so; at least it is not always so. (4) You challenge yourself that some truths find more credit with you than others. You do well; for God is true in the least as well as in the greatest, and he must be so to you. You must not call him true in one page of the leaf, and false in the other; for our Lord in all his writings never contradicted himself yet. Although the best of the regener-

[1] Without delay.

ate have slipped here, always labour you to hold your feet.

4. Comparing the state of one truly regenerate, whose heart is a temple of the Holy Ghost, and yours, which is full of uncleanness and corruption, you stand dumb and discouraged, and dare not sometimes call Christ heartsomely your own. I answer (1) The best regenerate have their defilements, that will clog behind them all their days; and wash as they will, there will be filth in their bosom. But let not this put you from the well. (2) Albeit there be some ounce-weights of carnality, and some squint-look or eye in our neck to an idol, yet love in its own measure may be sound. For glory must purify and perfect our love; it will never till then be absolutely pure. Yet if the idol reign, and have the yolk of the heart, and the keys of the house, and Christ only be made an underling to run errands, all is not right; therefore examine well. (3) There is a two-fold discouragement; one of unbelief, to conclude (and make doubt of the conclusion) for a mote in your eye, and a by-look to an idol; this is ill. There is another discouragement of sorrow for sin, when you find a by-look to an idol; this is good, and a matter of thanksgiving; therefore examine here also.

5. The assurance of Jesus's love, you say, would be the most comfortable news that ever you heard. Answer: That may stop twenty holes, and loose many objections; that love hath telling[1] in it, I trow. O that you knew and felt it, as I have done! I wish you a share of my feast; sweet, sweet hath it been to me. If my Lord had not given me this love, I should have fallen through the causeway of Aberdeen ere now. But for you, hang on, your feast is not far off; you shall be filled ere you go. There is as much in our Lord's pantry as will satisfy all his bairns, and as much wine in his cellar as will quench all their thirst. Hunger on, for there is meat in hunger for Christ; go never from him, but go to

[1]Something to mark down.

him (who yet is pleased with the importunity of hungry souls) with a dish-full of hungry desires, till he fill you. And if he delay, yet come not away, albeit you should fall a-swoon at his feet.

6. You crave my mind, whether sound comfort may be found in prayer, when conviction of a known idol is present. I answer, an idol, as an idol, cannot stand with sound comfort; for that comfort that is gotten at Dagon's feet is a cheat or blaflume.[1] Yet sound comfort, and conviction of an eye to an idol, may as well dwell together as tears and joy. But let this do you no ill; I speak it for your encouragement, that you may make the best of your joys you can, albeit you find them mixed with motes. Soul conviction, if alone, without remorse and grief, is not enough; therefore lend it a tear, if you are able to obtain it.

7. You question, when you obtain more fervency sometimes with your neighbour in prayer than when you are alone, whether hypocrisy be in it, or not? I answer, if this be always, no question a spice of hypocrisy is in it, which should be taken heed to. But possibly desertion may be in private, and presence in public, and then the case is clear. A fit of applause may occasion by accident a rubbing of a cold heart, and so heat and life may come; but it is not the proper cause of that heat. Hence God of his free grace will ride his errands upon our corruption. But corruption is but a mere occasion and accident, as the playing on a pipe removed anger from the prophet, and made him fitter to prophesy [2 *Kings* 3. 15].

8. You complain of Christ's short visits, that he will not bear you company one night; but when you lie down warm at night, you rise cold at morning. Answer: I cannot blame you, nor any other who knoweth that sweet Guest, for bemoaning his withdrawings, and being most desirous of his abode and company; for he would captivate and en-

[1] See *p* 115 *fn* 2.

gage the affection of any creature that saw his face. Since he looked on me, and gave me a sight of his fair love, he gained my heart wholly, and got away with it. Well, well may he brook[1] it! He shall keep it long ere I fetch it from him. But I will tell you what you should do; treat him well, give him the chair and the board-head, and make him welcome to the mean portion you have. A good supper and kind entertainment maketh the guest love the inn the better. Yet sometimes Christ hath an errand elsewhere, for mere trial;[2] and then, though you give him king's cheer, he will away; as is clear in desertions for mere trial and not for sin.

9. You seek the difference betwixt the motions of the Spirit, in their least measure, and the natural joys of your own heart. Answer: If you sorrow for any thing that may offend the Lord, it will speak the singleness of your love to him.

10. You ask the reason why sense overcometh faith. Answer: Because sense is more natural, and near of kin to our own selfish and soft nature. You ask if faith in that case be sound? Answer: If it be chased away, it is neither sound nor unsound, because it is not faith. But it might be, and was faith, before sense did blow out the act of believing.

11. You ask what to do, when promises are borne in upon you, and sense of impenitency for sins of youth hindereth application. Answer: If it be living sense, it may stand with application; and in this case, put to your hand and eat your meat in God's name. If false, so that the sins of youth are not repented of, then, as faith and impenitency cannot stand together, so neither that sense and application can consist.

[1] Enjoy, possess.   [2] That is, so that faith may be tried.

50/TO THOMAS CORBET

Godly counsels
Following Christ

Aberdeen, 1637

Dear Friend:

I forget you not. It will be my joy that you follow after Christ till you find him. My conscience is a feast of joy to me, that I sought in singleness of heart, for Christ's love, to put you upon the King's highway to our Bridegroom and our Father's house. Thrice blessed are you, my dear brother, if you hold the way.

I believe that you and Christ once met; I hope you will not sunder with him. Follow the counsel of the man of God, Mr William Dalgleish. If you depart from what I taught you in a hair-breadth, for fear or favour of men, or desire of ease in this world, I take heaven and earth to witness that ill shall come upon you in the end. Build not your nest here. This world is a hard, ill-made bed; no rest is in it for your soul. Awake, awake, and make haste to seek that Pearl, Christ, that this world seeth not. Your night and your Master Christ will be upon you within a clap; your hand-breadth of time will not bide you. Take Christ, howbeit a storm follow him. Howbeit this day be not yours and Christ's, the morrow will be yours and his. I would not exchange the joy of my bonds and imprisonment for Christ with all the joy of this dirty and foul-skinned world. I am filled with Christ's love.

I desire your wife to do what I write to you. Let her remember how dear Christ will be to her, when her breath turneth cold, and the eye-strings shall break. Oh how joyful should my soul be, to know that I had brought on a marriage betwixt Christ and that people, few or many. If it be not so, I shall be woe to be a witness against them. Use prayer: love not the world: be humble, and esteem little of yourself. Love your enemies and pray for them. Make conscience of speaking truth, when none knoweth but God. I never eat but I pray for you all. Pray for me. You and I shall see one another up in our Father's house. I rejoice to hear that your eye is upon Christ. Follow on, hang on, and quit him not. The Lord Jesus be with your spirit.

51/TO WILLIAM GLENDINNING

> *Sweetness of trial*
> *Swiftness of trial*
> *Prevalence of sin*

Aberdeen, 1637

Dear Brother:

Grace, mercy and peace be to you.

Your case is unknown to me, whether you be yet our Lord's prisoner at Wigtown or not. However it be, I know that our Lord Jesus hath been inquiring for you, and that he hath honoured you to bear his chains, which is the golden end of his cross, and so hath waled[1] out a chosen and honourable cross for you. I wish you much joy and comfort of it; for I have nothing to say of Christ's cross but much good. I hope that my ill word shall never meet either Christ or his sweet and easy cross. I know that he seeketh of us an outcast[2] with this house of clay, this mother prison, this earth that we love full well. And verily, when Christ snuffeth my candle and causeth my light to shine upward, it is one of my greatest

[1]Chosen. [2]Quarrel, contention.

wonders that dirt and clay hath so much court with a soul not made of clay; and that our soul goeth out of kind so far as to make an idol of this earth, such a deformed harlot, as that it should wrong Christ of our love.

How fast, how fast doth our ship sail! and how fair a wind hath time, to blow us off these coasts and this land of dying and perishing things! Alas! our ship saileth one way, and fleeth many miles in one hour, to hasten us upon eternity, and our love and hearts are sailing close backover[1] and swimming towards ease, lawless pleasure, vain honour, perishing riches; and to build a fool's nest I know not where, and to lay our eggs within the sea-mark, and fasten our bits of broken anchors upon the worst ground in the world, this fleeting and perishing life! And in the meanwhile, time and tide carry us upon another life, and there is daily less and less oil in our lamps, and less and less sand in our watchglass.[2] O what a wise course were it for use to look away from the false beauty of our borrowed prison, and to mind and eye and lust for our country! Lord, Lord, take us home!

And for myself: I think if a poor, weak, dying sheep seek for an old dyke and the lee-side of an hill in a storm, I have cause to long for a covert from this storm, in heaven. I know none will take my room over my head there. But certainly sleepy bodies would be at rest and a well-made bed, and an old crazed bark at a shore, and a wearied traveller at home, and a breathless horse at the rink's[3] end. I see nothing in this life but sin and the sour fruits of sin. And, oh, what a burden is sin! And what a slavery and miserable bondage is it, to be at the nod, and yeas and nays, of such a lord-master as a body of sin! Truly, when I think of it, it is a wonder that Christ maketh not fire and ashes of such a dry branch as I am. I would often lie down under Christ's feet and bid him trample upon me, when I consider my guiltiness. But seeing he hath sworn that sin shall not loose his unchangeable

[1]Backward. [2]Hour-glass. [3]Race-course.

covenant, I keep house-room amongst the rest of the ill-learned bairns, and must cumber the Lord of the house with the rest, till my Lord take the fetters off legs and arms, and destroy this body of sin, and make a hole or breach in this cage of earth, that the bird may fly out and the imprisoned soul be at liberty. In the meantime, the least intimation of Christ's love is sweet, and the hope of marriage with the Bridegroom holdeth me in some joyful on-waiting, that, when Christ's summer-birds shall sing upon the branches of the Tree of Life, I shall be tuned by God himself to help them to sing the home-coming of our Well-beloved and his bride to their house together. When I think of this, I think winters and summers, and years and days, and time, do me a pleasure that they shorten this untwisted and weak thread of my life, and that they put sin and miseries by-hand,[1] and that they shall carry me to my Bridegroom in a clap.[2]

Dear brother, pray for me, that it would please the Lord of the vineyard to give me room to preach his righteousness again to the great congregation. Grace, grace be with you. Remember me to your wife.

52/TO MARION M'NAUGHT

A spring-tide of Christ's love

Aberdeen, 22 November 1637

My dear and well-beloved Sister:

Grace, mercy and peace be to you.

I am well, honour to God. I have been before a court set up within me of terrors and challenges, but my sweet Lord Jesus

[1]Aside. [2]That is, on a sudden (as when thunder is heard).

hath taken the mask off his face and said, 'Kiss thy fill!'; and I will not smother nor conceal the kindness of my King Jesus. He hath broken in upon the poor prisoner's soul like the swelling of Jordan. I am bank and brim full, a great high spring-tide of the consolations of Christ have overflowed me. I would not give my weeping for the fourteen prelates' laughter. They have sent me here to feast with my King. His spikenard casteth a sweet smell. The Bridegroom's love hath run away with my heart. O love, love, love! O sweet are my royal King's chains! I care not for fire nor torture. How sweet were it to me to swim the salt sea for my new Lover, my second Husband, my first Lord! I charge you in the name of God not to fear the wild beasts that entered into the vineyard of the Lord of hosts. The false prophet is the tail. God shall cut the tail from Scotland. Take your comfort and droop not, despond not.

Pray for my poor flock; I would take a penance on my soul for their salvation. I fear that the entering of a hireling upon my labours there will cut off my life with sorrow. There I wrestled with the Angel and prevailed. Wood, trees, meadows and hills are my witnesses that I drew on a fair meeting betwixt Christ and Anwoth.

My love to your husband, to dear Carleton, to my beloved brother Knockbrex. Forget not Christ's prisoner. I long for a letter under your own hand.

53/TO JOHN GORDON

> *Heaven hard to be won*
> *Many come short of attaining*
> *Idol sins to be renounced*
> *Likeness to Christ*

Aberdeen, 1637

Dear Brother:

I earnestly desire to know the case of your soul and to understand that you have made sure work of heaven and salvation.

1. Remember that salvation is one of Christ's dainties which he giveth but to a few.

2. That it is violent sweating and striving that taketh heaven.

3. That it cost Christ's blood to purchase that house to sinners, and to set mankind down as the King's free tenants and freeholders.

4. That many make a start toward heaven who fall on their back and win not up to the top of the mount. It plucketh heart and legs from them, and they sit down and give it over, because the devil setteth a sweet-smelled flower to their nose (this fair busked[1] world) wherewith they are bewitched, and so forget or refuse to go forward.

5. Remember that many go far on and reform many things, and can find tears, as Esau did; and suffer hunger for truth, as Judas did; and wish and desire the end of the righteous, as Balaam did; and profess fair, and fight for the Lord, as Saul did; and desire the saints of God to pray for them, as Pharaoh and Simon Magus did; and prophesy and speak of Christ, as Caiaphas did; and walk softly and mourn for fear of judgments, as Ahab did; and put away gross sins

[1] Adorned.

and idolatry, as Jehu did; and hear the Word of God gladly, and reform their life in many things according to the Word, as Herod did; and say to Christ, 'Master, I will follow thee whithersoever thou goest', as the man who offered to be Christ's servant did [*Matt* 8. 19]. And many may taste of the virtues of the life to come, and be partaker of the wonderful gifts of the Holy Ghost, and taste of the good Word of God, as did the apostates who sin against the Holy Ghost [*Heb* 6]. And yet all these are but like gold in clink and colour, and watered brass, and base metal. These are written that we should try ourselves, and not rest till we be a step nearer Christ than sunburnt and withering professors can come.

6. Consider that it is impossible that your idol-sins and you can go to heaven together; and that they who will not part with these can, indeed, love Christ at the bottom, but only in word and show, which will not do the business.

7. Remember how swiftly God's post time flieth away, and that your forenoon is already spent, your afternoon will come, and then your evening, and at last night, when you cannot see to work. Let your heart be set upon finishing of your journey, and summing and laying your accounts with your Lord. O how blessed shall you be to have a joyful welcome of your Lord at night! How blessed are they who, in time, take sure course with their souls! Bless his great name for what you possess in goods and children, ease and worldly contentment, that he hath given you; and seek to be like Christ in humility and lowliness of mind. And be not great and entire with the world. Make it not your god, nor your lover that you trust unto, for it will deceive you.

I recommend Christ and his love to you, in all things. Let him have the flower of your heart and your love. Set a low price upon all things but Christ, and cry down in your thoughts clay and dirt, that will not comfort you when you get summons to remove, and appear before your Judge to answer for all the deeds done in the body. The Lord give you wisdom in all things. I beseech you sanctify God in your speaking, for holy and reverend is his name; and be temperate and sober. Companionry with the bad is a sin that holdeth many out of heaven.

I will not believe that you will receive the ministry of a stranger, who will preach a new and uncouth doctrine to you. Let my salvation stand for it, if I delivered not the plain and whole counsel of God to you in his Word. Read this letter to your wife, and remember my love to her, and request her to take heed to do what I write to you. I pray for you and yours. Remember me in your prayers to our Lord, that he would be pleased to send me amongst you again. Grace be with you.

Your lawful and loving pastor.

S.R

54/TO THE PARISHIONERS OF KILMACOLM

Spiritual sloth
Advice to beginners
A dead ministry
Languor
Obedience
Want of Christ's felt presence
Assurance important
Prayer-meetings

Anwoth, 5 August 1639[1]

Worthy and well-beloved in Christ Jesus our Lord:

Grace, mercy and peace be to you. Your letters could not come to my hand in a greater throng of business than I am now pressed with at this time, when our Kirk requireth the public help of us all; yet I cannot but answer the heads of both your letters, with provision that ye choose, after this, a fitter time for writing.

I would not have you pitch upon me as the man able by letters to answer doubts of this kind, while there are in your bounds men of such great parts, most able for this work. I know that the best are unable; yet it pleaseth that Spirit of Jesus to blow his sweet wind through a piece of dry stick, that the empty reed may keep no glory to itself. But a minister can make no such wind as this to blow; he is scarce able to lend it a passage to blow through him.

Know that the wind of this Spirit hath a time when it bloweth sharp, and pierceth so strongly, that it would blow through an iron door; and this is commonly rather under suffering for Christ than at any other time. Sick children get

[1] After spending eighteen months in exile at Aberdeen, Rutherford took advantage of 'the covenanting revolution' of 1638 to return to Anwoth.

of Christ's pleasant things to play with, because Jesus is most
tender of the sufferer, for he was a sufferer himself. O if I had
but the leavings and the drawing of the by-board[1] of a
sufferer's table! But I leave this to answer yours.

I. You write that God's vows are lying on you, and security
strong, and sib[2] to nature stealing on you who are weak. I
answer:

1. Till we be in heaven, the best have heavy heads, as is
   evident [*Cant* 5. 2; *Psalm* 30. 6; *Job* 29. 18; *Matt* 26. 43].
   Nature is a sluggard, and loveth not the labour of religion.
   Therefore rest should not be taken till we know the
   disease be over, and in the way of turning, and that it is
   like a fever past the cool. And the quietness and the calms
   of the faith of victory over corruption should be entertained in place of security; so that if I sleep, I would
   desire to sleep faith's sleep in Christ's bosom.

2. Know also, none that sleep sound can seriously complain
   of sleepiness. Sorrow for a slumbering soul is a token of
   some watchfulness of spirit. But this is soon turned into
   wantonness, as grace in us too often is abused. Therefore
   our waking must be watched over, else sleep will even
   grow out of watching; and there is as much need to watch
   over grace as to watch over sin. Full men will soon sleep,
   and sooner than hungry men.

3. For your weakness to keep off security, that like a thief
   stealeth upon you, I would say two things: 1. To want
   complaints of weakness, is for heaven, and angels that
   never sinned, not for Christians in Christ's camp on earth.
   I think our weakness maketh us the church of the redeemed ones, and Christ's field that the Mediator should
   labour in. If there were no diseases on earth, there needed
   no physicians on earth. If Christ had cried down weakness,
   he might have cried down his own calling. But weakness
   is our Mediator's world: sin is Christ's only fair and

[1]Side-table where children sat.   [2]Akin.

market. No man should rejoice at weakness and diseases; but I think we may have a sort of gladness at boils and sores, because without them, Christ's fingers (as a slain Lord) should never have touched our skin. I dare not thank myself, but I dare thank God's depth of wise providence, that I have an errand in me, while I live, for Christ to come and visit me, and bring with him his drugs and his balm. O how sweet is it for a sinner to put his weakness in Christ's strengthening hand, and to take a sick soul to such a Physician, and to lay weakness before him, to weep upon him, and to plead and pray! Weakness can speak and cry, when we have not a tongue. 'And when I passed by thee, and saw thee polluted in thine own blood, I said unto thee, when thou wast in thy blood, Live' [*Ezek* 16. 6]. The kirk could not speak one word to Christ then; but blood and guiltiness out of measure spake, and drew out of Christ pity, and a word of life and love. 2. As for weakness, we have it that we may employ Christ's strength because of our weakness. Weakness is to make us the strongest things; that is, when, having no strength of our own, we are carried upon Christ's shoulders, and walk, as it were, upon his legs. If our sinful weakness swell up to the clouds, Christ's strength will swell up to the sun, and far above the heaven of heavens.

II. You tell me, that there is need of counsel for strengthening new beginners. I can say little to that, who am not well begun myself; but I know honest beginnings are nourished by him, even by lovely Jesus, who never yet put out a poor man's dim candle, who is wrestling betwixt light and darkness. I am sure if new beginners would urge themselves upon Christ, and press their souls upon him, and importune him for a draught of his sweet love, they could not come wrong to Christ. Come once in upon the right step of his lovely love, and I defy you to get free of him again. If any beginners fall off Christ again, and miss him, they never lighted upon Christ as Christ; it was but an idol, like Jesus, which they took for him.

III. Whereas you complain of a dead ministry in your bounds: you are to remember that the Bible among you is the contract of marriage; and the manner of Christ's conveying his love to your heart is not so absolutely dependent upon even lively preaching, as that there is no conversion at all, no life of God, but that which is tied to a man's lips. The daughters of Jerusalem have done often that which the watchmen could not do. Make Christ your minister. He can woo a soul at a dyke-side in the field. He needeth not us, howbeit the flock be obliged to seek him in the shepherds' tents. Hunger of Christ's making may thrive even under stewards who mind not the feeding of the flock. O blessed soul that can leap over a man, and look above a pulpit, up to Christ, who can preach home to the heart, howbeit we were all dead and rotten!

IV. So to complain of yourselves as to justify God is right, providing ye justify his Spirit in yourselves. For men seldom advocate against Satan's work and sin in themselves, but against God's work in themselves. Some of the people of God slander God's grace in their souls, as some wretches used to do, who complain and murmur of want. ('I have nothing', say they, 'all is gone, the ground yieldeth but weeds and windle-straws'[1]) when their fat harvest and their money in bank maketh them liars. But for myself, alas! I think it is not my sin; I have scarce wit to sin this sin. But I advise you to speak good of Christ for his beauty and sweetness, and speak good of him for his grace to yourselves.

V. Light remaineth, you say, but you cannot attain to painfulness. See if this complaint be not booked in the New Testament: and the place [*Rom* 7. 18] is like this, 'To will is present with me; but how to perform that which is good, I find not'. But every one hath not Paul's spirit in complaining: for often in us complaining is but a humble backbiting and

[1]See p 41 *fn* 1.

traducing of Christ's new work in the soul. But for the matter of the complaint, I would say that the light of glory is perfectly obeyed in loving and praising and rejoicing and resting in a seen and known Lord. But that light is not hereaway in any clay-body; for, while we are here, light is, in the most, broader and longer than our narrow and feckless[1] obedience. But if there be light, with a fair train and a great back (I mean, armies) of challenging thoughts, and sorrow for coming short of performance in what we know and see ought to be performed, then that sorrow for not doing is accepted of our Lord for doing. Our honest sorrow and sincere aims, together with Christ's intercession, pleading that God would welcome that which we have and forgive what we have not, must be our life, till we be over the bound-road,[2] and in the other country, where the law will get a perfect soul.

VI. In Christ's absence there is, as you write, a willingness to use means, but heaviness after the use of them, because of formal and slight performance. In Christ's absence, I confess, the work lieth behind. But if you mean absence of comfort, and absence of sense of his sweet presence, I think that absence is Christ's trying of us, not simply our sin against him. Therefore, howbeit our obedience be not sugared and sweetened with joy, which is the sweet-meat bairns would still be at, yet the less sense and the more willingness in obeying, the less formality in our obedience. Howbeit we think not so; for I believe that many think obedience formal and lifeless, except the wind be fair in the west, and sails filled with joy and sense, till souls, like a ship fair before the wind, can spread no more sail. But I am not of their mind who think so. But if you mean, by absence of Christ, the withdrawing of his working grace, I see not how willingness to use means can be at all under such an absence. Therefore be humbled for heaviness in that obedience, and thankful for willingness; for the Bride-

---

[1] See p40 fn 1. [2] That is, the boundry (between earth and heaven).

groom is busking[1] his spouse oftentimes while she is half
sleeping; and your Lord is working and helping more than
you see. Also I recommend to you heaviness for formality, and
for lifeless deadness in obedience. Be cast down, as much as
you will or can, for deadness; and challenge that slow and dull
carcase of sin that will neither lead nor drive, in your spiritual
obedience. O how sweet to lovely Jesus are bills and griev-
ances given in against corruption and the body of sin! I would
have Christ, in such a case, fashed,[2] if I may speak so, and
deafened with our cries, as you see the apostle doth [*Rom* 7. 24]:
'O wretched man that I am! who shall deliver me from the
body of this death?' Protestations against the law of sin in
you are law-grounds why sin can have no law against you.
Seek to have your protestation discussed and judged, and then
shall you find Christ on your side of it.

VII. You hold that Christ must either have hearty service
or no service at all. If you mean he will not have a heart, or
feigned service such as the hypocrites give him, I grant you
that Christ must have honesty or nothing. But if you mean
that he will have no service at all where the heart draweth
back in any measure, I would not that were true for my part
of heaven, and all that I am worth in the world. If you mind
to walk to heaven without a cramp or a crook, I fear you must
go alone. He knoweth our dross and defects, and pitieth us,
when weakness and deadness in our obedience is our cross,
and not our darling.

VIII. The liar [*John* 8. 44], as you write, challengeth the
work as formal; yet you bless your Cautioner[3] for the
ground-work he hath laid, and dare not say but that you have
assurance in some measure. To this I say:

1. It shall be no fault to save Satan's labour, and challenge it
   yourselves, or at least examine and censure. But beware of
   Satan's ends in challenging, for he mindeth to put Christ

[1]See *p* 152 *for* 1. [2] Troubled. [3] See *p* 50 *fn* 2.

and you at odds.

2. Welcome home faith in Jesus, who washeth still, when we have defiled our souls and made ourselves loathsome; and seek still the blood of atonement for faults little or meikle.[1] Know the gate to the well, and lie about it.

3. Make meikle[1] of assurance, for it keepeth your anchor fixed.

IX. Out-breakings, you say, discourage you, so that you know not if ever you shall arrive again at such overjoying consolations of the Spirit in this life, as formerly you had; and therefore a question may be, If, after assurance and mortification, the children of God be ordinarily fed with sense and joy? I answer, I see no inconvenience to think it is enough, in a race, to see the goal at the starting place, howbeit the runners never get a view of it till they come to the rink's[2] end; and that our wise Lord thinketh it fittest we should not always be fingering and playing with Christ's apples. Our Well-beloved, I know, will sport and play with his bride, as much as he thinketh will allure her to the rink's end. Yet I judge it not unlawful to seek renewed consolations, providing,

1. The heart be submissive, and content to leave the measure and timing of them to him.

2. They be sought to excite us to praise, and to strengthen our assurance, and sharpen our desires after himself.

3. They be sought, not for our humours or swelling of nature, but as the earnest of heaven. And I think, many do attain to greater consolations after mortification, than ever they had formerly. But I know that our Lord walketh here still by a sovereign latitude, and keepeth not the same way, as to one hair-breadth without a miss, towards all his children.

As for the Lord's people with you, I am not the man fit to speak to them. I rejoice exceedingly that Christ is engaging souls amongst you: but I know that, in conversion, all the

[1]Much. [2]See p 149 fn 3.

winning is in the first buying, as we use to say. For many lay false foundations, and take up conversion at their foot, and get Christ for as good as half-nothing, and had never a sick night for sin, and this maketh loose work. I pray you dig deep. Christ's palace-work, and his new dwelling, laid upon hell felt and feared, is most firm: and heaven, grounded and laid upon such a hell, is surest work, and will not wash away with winter-storms. It were good that professors were not like young heirs, that come to their rich estate long ere they come to their wit; and so the tavern, and the cards, and harlots steal their riches from them ere they be aware what they are doing. I know that a Christ bought with strokes is sweetest.

I recommend to you conference and prayer at private meetings. For warrant whereof, see *Is* 2. 3; *Jer* 50. 4, 5; *Hos* 2. 1, 2; *Zech* 8. 20-23; *Mal* 3. 16; *Luke* 24. 13-17; *John* 20. 19; *Acts* 12. 12; *Col* 3. 16 and 4. 6; *Eph* 4. 29; 1 *Pet* 4. 10; 1 *Thess* 5. 14; *Heb* 3. 13 and 10. 25. Many coals make a good fire, and that is a part of the communion of saints.

I must entreat you, and your Christian acquaintances in the parish, to remember me to God in your prayers, and my flock and ministry, and my transportation and removal from this place, which I fear at this Assembly:[1] and be earnest with God for our mother-kirk. For want of time, I have put you all in one letter. The rich grace of our Lord Jesus Christ be with you all.

[1] After returning to Anwoth, Rutherford received two calls: (1) to minister at Edinburgh, (2) to accept a theological chair in the University of St Andrews. The Assembly mentioned in the letter was held at Glasgow. It invited Rutherford to accept the call to St Andrews. He agreed to do so, but reluctantly.

55/TO ALEXANDER LEIGHTON
Christ's prisoner in bonds at London
Public blessings alleviate private sufferings
Trials light when viewed in the light of heaven
Christ worthy of his people's sufferings

St Andrews, 22 November 1639

Rev. and much honoured prisoner of hope:

Grace, mercy and peace be to you; it was not my part, whom our Lord hath enlarged, to forget you his prisoner. When I consider how long your night hath been, I think Christ hath a mind to put you, in free grace's debt, so much the deeper, as your sufferings have been of so long a continuance. But what if Christ intend you no joy but public joy, with enlarged and triumphing Zion? I think, sir, that you would love it best, to share and divide your song of joy with Zion; and to have mystical Christ in Britain partner with your enlargement. I am sure, your joy, bordering and neighbouring with the joy of Christ's bride, would be so much the sweeter that it were public. I thought, if Christ had halved my mercies, and delivered his bride and not me, that his praises should have been double to what they are; but now two rich mercies, conjoined in one, have stolen from our Lord more than half-praises. O, that mercy should so beguile us, and steal away our accounts and acknowledgments!

Worthy sir, I hope that I need not exhort you to go on in hoping for the salvation of God. There hath not been so much taken from your time of ease and created joys as eternity shall add to your heaven. You know, when one day in heaven hath paid you, yea, and overpaid your blood, bonds, sorrow and sufferings, that it would trouble an angel's understanding to lay the account of that surplus of glory which eternity can and will give you. O, but your sand-glass of sufferings and losses cometh to little, when it shall be counted and compared with the glory that abideth you on the other side of the water! You have no leisure to rejoice and sing here, while time goeth about you, and where your psalms will be short; therefore you will think eternity and the long day of heaven, that shall be measured with no other sun nor horologue[1] than the long life of the 'Ancient of days' to measure your praises, little enough for you. If your span-length of time be cloudy, you cannot but think your Lord can no more take your blood and your bands without the income and recompense of free grace, than he would take the sufferings of Paul, and his other dear servants, that were well paid home beyond all counting [*Rom* 8, 18].

If the wisdom of Christ hath made you Anti-christ's eye-sore, and his envy, you are to thank God that such a piece of clay as you are is made the field of glory to work upon. It was the Potter's aim that the clay should praise him; and I hope it satisfieth you that your clay is for his glory. Oh, who can suffer enough for such a Lord! and who can lay out in bank enough of pain, shame, losses, torture, to receive in again the free interest of eternal glory? [2 *Cor* 4, 17]. O, how advantageous a bargaining is it with such a rich Lord! If your hand and pen had been at leisure to gain glory on paper, it had been but paper-glory; but the bearing of a public cross so long, for the now controverted privileges of the crown and sceptre of free King Jesus, the Prince of the kings of the earth, is glory booked in heaven.

Worthy and dear brother, if you weigh Jesus' sweetness, excellency, glory and beauty, and lay foregainst[2] him your ounces or drachms of suffering for him, you will be straitened two ways,

---

[1] See p 138 *fn* 2.
[2] Opposite.

1. It will be a pain to make the comparison, the disproportion being by no understanding imaginable: nay, if heaven's arithmetic and angels were set to work, they should never number the degrees of difference.

2. It would straiten you to find a scale for the balance to put in that high and lofty One, that over-transcending Prince of excellency. If your mind could fancy as many created heavens as time hath had minutes, trees have had leaves, and clouds have had raindrops, since the first stone of the creation was laid, they would not make half a scale to bear and weigh boundless excellency. And therefore the King, whose marks you are bearing, and whose dying you carry about with you in your body is, out of all cry and consideration, beyond and above all our thoughts. For myself, I am content to feed upon wondering sometimes, at beholding but the borders and skirts of the incomparable glory which is in that exalted Prince. I think you could wish for more ears[1] to give him than you have, since you hope these ears you now have given him shall be passages to take in the music of his glorious voice.

I would fain both believe and pray for a new bride of Jews and Gentiles to our Lord Jesus, after the land of graven images shall be laid waste; and that our Lord Jesus is on horseback, hunting and pursuing the beast; and that England and Ireland shall be well-swept chambers for Christ and his righteousness to dwell in; for he hath opened our graves in Scotland, and the two dead and buried witnesses are risen again, and are prophesying. O, that princes would glory in carrying the train of Christ's robe-royal in their arms! Let me die within half an hour after I have seen the Son of God's temple enlarged, and the cords of Jerusalem's tent lengthened, to take in a more numerous company for a bride to the Son of God! O, if the corner or foundation-stone of that house, that new house, were laid above my grave!

[1] Leighton's ears had been cut off by his persecutors.

O! who can add to him, who is that great All! If he would create suns and moons, new heavens, thousand thousand degrees more perfect than these that now are; and again, make a new creation ten thousand thousand degrees in perfection beyond that new creation; and again, still for eternity multiply new heavens; they should never be a perfect resemblance of that infinite excellency, order, weight, measure, beauty and sweetness that is in him. O how little of him do we see! O how shallow are our thoughts of him! O if I had pain for him, and shame and losses for him, and more clay and spirits for him! and that I could go upon earth without love, desire, hope, because Christ hath taken away my love, desire and hope to heaven with him! I know, worthy sir, your sufferings for him are your glory: and therefore, weary not; his salvation is near at hand, and shall not tarry. Pray for me. His grace be with you.

56/TO JAMES WILSON

Advices to a doubting soul
Mistakes about an interest in God's love
Temptation
Perplexity about prayer
Want of feeling

St Andrews, 8 January 1640

Dear Brother:

Grace, mercy and peace be multiplied upon you. I bless our rich and only wise Lord, who careth so for his new creation that he is going over it again, and trying every piece in you, and blowing away the motes of his new work in you. Alas! I am not so fit a physician as your disease requireth: sweet,

sweet, lovely Jesus be your physician, where his under-surgeons cannot do anything for putting in order the wheels, paces and goings of a marred soul. I have little time: but yet the Lord hath made me so concern myself in your condition, that I cannot, I dare not be altogether silent.

You doubt from 2 *Cor* 13, 5, whether you be in Christ or not? and so, whether you be a reprobate or not? I answer three things to the doubt.

1. You owe charity to all men, but most of all to lovely and loving Jesus, and some also to yourself, especially to your renewed self; because your new self is not yours, but another Lord's, even the work of his own Spirit: therefore, to slander his work is to wrong himself. Love thinketh no evil; if you love grace, think not ill of grace in yourself. And you think ill of grace in yourself when you make it but a bastard and a work of nature. For a holy fear that you be not Christ's, and withal a care and a desire to be his, and not your own, is not, nay, cannot be bastard nature. The great Advocate pleadeth hard for you; be upon the Advocate's side, O poor fearful client of Christ. Stay and side with such a lover, who pleadeth for no other man's goods but his own; for he (if I may say so) scorneth to be enriched with an unjust conquest. And yet he pleadeth for you, whereof your letter, though too, too full of jealousy, is a proof. For if you were not his, your thoughts (which I hope are but the suggestions of his Spirit, that only bringeth the matter in debate, to make it sure to you) would not be such, nor so serious, as these, 'Am I his?' or, 'Whose am I?'

2. Dare you forswear your Owner and say in cold blood, 'I am not his?' What nature or corruption saith at starts in you, I regard not. Your thoughts of yourself, when sin and guiltiness round[1] you in the ear, and when you have a sight of your deservings, are Apocrypha, and not Scripture,

[1]Whisper.

I hope. Hear what the Lord saith of you, 'He will speak peace'. If your Master say, 'I quit you', I shall then bid you eat ashes for bread, and drink waters of gall and wormwood. But howbeit Christ out of his own mouth should seem to say, 'I come not for thee', as he did [*Matt* 15. 24], yet let me say that the words of tempting Jesus[1] are not to be stretched as Scripture beyond his intention, seeing his intention in speaking them is to strengthen, not to deceive. And therefore here faith may contradict what Christ seemeth at first to say, and so may you. I charge you, by the mercies of God, be not so cruel to grace and the new birth as to cast water on your own coal by misbelief. If you must die (as I know you shall not), it were a folly to slay yourself.

3. I hope that you love the new birth and a claim to Christ, howbeit you do not make it good; and if you were in hell, and saw the heavenly face of lovely, ten thousand times lovely Jesus, that hath God's hue, and God's fair, fair and comely red and white, wherewith it is beautified beyond comparison and imagination, you could not forbear to say, 'Oh, if I could but blow a kiss from my sinful mouth, from hell up to heaven, upon his cheeks that are a bed of spices, as sweet flowers!' [*Cant* 5. 13]. I hope you dare say, 'O fairest sight of heaven! O boundless mass of crucified and slain love for me, give me leave to wish to love thee! O Flower and Bloom of heaven and earth's love! O angel's wonder! O thou, the Father's eternal sealed love! And O thou, God's eternal delight, give me leave to stand beside thy love, and look in and wonder, and give me leave to wish to love thee, if I can do no more.'

We being born in atheism, and bairns of the house that we are come of, it is no new thing, my dear brother, for us to be under jealousies and mistakes about the love of God. What think you of this, that the man Christ was tempted to believe

[1]That is, when the Lord puts the soul on trial.

there were but two Persons in the blessed God-head, and that
the Son of God, the substantial and co-eternal Son, was not the
lawful Son of God? Did not Satan say, 'If thou be the Son of
God?'

You say, that you know not what to do. Your Head said
once that same word, or not far from it [*John* 12, 27]: 'Now is
my soul troubled; and what shall I say?' And faith answered
Christ's 'What shall I say?' with these words, 'O tempted
Saviour, askest thou, "What shall I say?" Say, "Pray, Father,
save me from this hour". ' What course can you take, but
pray, and trust Christ's own comforts? He is no bankrupt,
take his word.

'Oh,' say you, 'I cannot pray.' I answer, honest sighing is
faith breathing and whispering in the ear. The life is not out of
faith where there is sighing, looking up with the eyes, and
breathing toward God, 'Hide not thine ear at my breathing'
[*Lam* 3, 56].

'But what shall I do in spiritual exercises?' you say. I
answer:

1. If you knew particularly what to do, it were not a spiritual
   exercise.

2. In my weak judgment, you would first say, 'I will glorify
   God in believing David's salvation, and the Bride's
   marriage with the Lamb, and love the church's slain
   Husband, although I cannot for the present believe mine
   own salvation'.

3. Say, 'I will not pass from my claim; suppose Christ would
   pass from his claim to me, it shall not go back upon my
   side. Howbeit my love to him be not worth a drink of
   water, yet Christ shall have it, such as it is?'

4. Say, 'I shall rather spoil twenty prayers, than not pray at
   all. Let my broken words go up to heaven; when they
   come up into the great angel's golden censer, that com-
   passionate Advocate will put together my broken prayers

and perfume them.' Words are but the accidents[1] of prayer.

'Oh' say you, 'I am slain with hardness of heart, and troubled with confused and melancholy thoughts.' I answer:

1. My dear brother, would you conclude thence that you know not well who owneth you? I grant that, 'Oh, my heart is hard! oh my thoughts of faithless sorrow! therefore I know not who owneth me', were good logic in heaven amongst angels and the glorified. But down in Christ's hospital, where sick and distempered souls are under cure, it is not worth a straw. Give Christ time to end his work in your heart. Hold on in feeling and bewailing your hardness, for that is softness to feel hardness.

2. I charge you to make psalms of Christ's praises for his begun work of grace. Make Christ your music and your song; for complaining and feeling of want doth often swallow up your praises. What think you of those who go to hell never troubled with such thoughts? If your exercise be the way to hell, God help me! I have a cold coal to blow at, and a blank paper for heaven. I give you Christ's caution, and my heaven surety, for your salvation. Lend Christ your melancholy, for Satan hath no right to make chamber in your melancholy. Borrow joy and comfort from the Comforter. Bid the Spirit do his office in you; and remember that faith is one thing, and the feeling and notice of faith another. God forbid that this were good reasoning, 'No feeling, no grace'. I am sure, you were not always, these twenty years by-past, actually knowing that you live; yet all this time you are living; so is it with the life of faith.

But alas! dear brother, it is easy for me to speak words and syllables of peace, but Isaiah telleth you, 'I create peace' (57. 19). There is but one Creator, you know. Oh, that you may get a letter of peace sent you from heaven! Pray for

[1] Incidental accompaniments.

me, and for grace to be faithful, and gifts to be able with tongue and pen to glorify God. I forget you not.

57/TO DAVID DICKSON

[*On the death of a son*]

God's sovereignty
Discipline by affliction

St Andrews, 28 May 1640

Reverend and dear Brother:

You look like the house whereof you are a branch; the cross is a part of the life-rent that lieth to all the sons of the house. I desire to suffer with you, if I could take a lift of your house-trial off you; but you have preached it ere I knew anything of God.

Your Lord may gather his roses, and shake his apples, at what season of the year he pleaseth. Each husbandman cannot make harvest when he pleaseth, as the Lord can do. You are taught to know and adore his sovereignty which he exerciseth over you, which yet is lustred with mercy. The child hath but changed a bed in the garden, and is planted up higher, nearer the sun, where he shall thrive better than in this out-field moorground. You must think your Lord would not want him one hour longer; and since the date of your loan of him was expired (as it is, if you read the lease), let him have his own with gain, as good reason were. I read on it an exaltation and a richer measure of grace, as the sweet fruit of your cross: and I am bold to say, that that college,[1] where your Master hath set you now, shall find it.

[1] He had recently been appointed to a professorship of divinity in the University of Glasgow.

I am content that Christ is so homely with my dear brother, David Dickson, as to borrow and lend, and take and give with him. And you know what are called the visitations of such a friend; it is to come to the house and be homely with what is yours. I persuade myself upon his credit that he hath left a blessing, and that he hath made the house the better. I envy not[1] his waking love, who saw that this water was to be passed through, and that now the number of crosses lying in your way to glory are fewer by one than when I saw you. They must decrease. It is better than any ancient or modern commentary on your text that you preach upon, in Glasgow. Read and spell right, for he knoweth what he doeth. He is only lopping and snedding[2] a fruitful tree, that it may be more fruitful.

I congratulate heartily with you his new welcome to your new charge. Dearest brother, go on and faint not. Something of yours is in heaven, beside the flesh of your exalted Saviour, and you go on after your own. Time's thread is shorter by one inch than it was. An oath is sworn and past the seals, whether afflictions will or not, you must grow and swell out of your shell, and live, and triumph, and resign, and be more than a conqueror; for your Captain, who leadeth you on, is more than conqueror, and he makes you partaker of his conquest and victory. Did not love to you compel me, I would not fetch water to the well, and speak to one who knoweth better than I can do what God is doing with him. Remember my love to your wife, to Mr. John, and all friends there. Let us be helped by your prayers, for I cease not to make mention of you to the Lord, as I can. Grace be with you.

[1] That is, fret not at.
[2] Pruning.

58/TO LADY BOYD

Proceedings of the Westminster Assembly

London, 25 May 1644

Madam:

Grace, mercy and peace be to you. I received your letter on May 19th. We are here debating, with much contention of disputes, for the just measures of the Lord's temple. It pleaseth God that sometimes enemies hinder the building of the Lord's house; but now friends, even gracious men (so I conceive of them), do not a little hinder the work. Thomas Goodwin, Jeremiah Burroughs, and some others, four or five, who are for the Independent way, stand in our way, and are mighty opposites to presbyterial government. We have carried through some propositions for the Scripture right of presbytery, especially in the Church of Jerusalem [*Acts* 2, 4-6 and 15] and the church of Ephesus, and are going on upon other grounds of truth; and by the way have proven that ordination of pastors belongeth not to a single congregation, but to a college of presbyters, whose it is to lay hands upon Timothy and others [1 *Tim* 4. 14; 5. 17; *Acts* 13. 1, 2, 3; 6. 5, 6.] We are to prove that one single congregation hath not power to excommunicate, which is opposed not only by Independent men but by many others.

The truth is, we have at times grieved spirits with the work; and for my part, I often despair of the reformation of this land, which saw never anything but the high places of their fathers and the remnants of Babylon's pollutions. And except that, 'not by might, nor by power, but by the Spirit of the Lord', I should think God hath not yet thought it time for England's deliverance. For the truth is, the best of them almost have said, 'A half reformation is very fair at the first'; which is no other thing than, 'It is not time yet to build the house of the Lord'. And for that cause, many houses, great and fair in the land, are laid desolate.

Multitudes of Anabaptists, Antinomians, Familists, Separatists are here. The best of the people are of the Independent way. As for myself, I know no more if there be a sound Christian (setting aside some, yea, not a few learned, some zealous and faithful ministers whom I have met with) at London (though I doubt not but there are many), than if I were in Spain; which maketh me bless God that the communion of saints, how desirable soever, yet is not the thing, even that great thing, Christ and the remission of sins. If Jesus were unco,[1] as his members are here, I should be in a sad and heavy condition.

The House of Peers are rotten men, and hate our Commissioners and our cause both. The life that is, is in the House of Commons, and many of them also have their religion to choose. The sorrows of a travailing women are come on the land. Our army is lying about York, and have blocked up them of Newcastle, and six thousand Papists and Malignants, with Mr Thomas Sydserf and some Scottish prelates; and if God deliver them into their hands (considering how strong the Parliament's armies are, how many victories God hath given them since they entered into covenant with him, and how weak the King is), it may be thought the land is near a deliverance.[2] But I rather desire it than believe it.

We offered this day to the Assembly a part of a Directory for worship, to shoulder out the Service-Book. It is taken into consideration by the Assembly.

Your son Lindsay is well: I receive letters from him almost every week.

[1] See p 43 *fn* 2.
[2] The Parliamentary victory at Marston Moor followed on 2 July, 1644.

59/TO LADY KENMURE

Westminster Assembly
Religious sects

London, 4 March 1644

Madam:

Grace, mercy and peace be to you.

I am glad to hear that your Ladyship is in any tolerable health, and shall pray that the Lord may be your strength and rock. Sure I am that he took you out of the womb, and you have been cast on him from the breasts. I am confident that he will not leave you till he crown the work begun in you.

There is nothing here but divisions in the Church and Assembly; for beside Brownists and Independents (who, of all that differ from us, come nearest to walkers with God), there are many other sects here, of Anabaptists, Libertines who are for all opinions in religion, fleshly and abominable Antinomians, and Seekers, who are for no church ordinances, but expect apostles to come and reform churches; and a world of others, all against the government of presbyteries. Luther observed, when he studied to reform, that two-and-thirty sundry sects arose, of all which I have named a part, except those called Seekers who were not then arisen. He said, God should crush them, and that they should rise again; both which we see accomplished.

In the Assembly we have well near ended the government, and are upon the power of Synods, and I hope near at an end with them; and so I trust to be delivered from this prison shortly. The King hath dissolved the treaty of peace at Uxbridge,[1] and adhereth to his sweet prelates, and would abate

[1] During the Civil War of 1642-46 between the King on the one hand, and the Long Parliament and the Scots on the other, negotiations for peace took place at Uxbridge (16 miles N.W. of London), but on 22 February, 1645, they finally broke down.

nothing but a little of the rigour of their courts, and a suspending of laws against the ceremonies, not a taking away of them. The not prospering of our armies there in Scotland is ascribed here to the sins of the land, and particularly to the divisions and backslidings of many from the cause, and the not executing of justice against bloody malignants.

My wife here, under the physicians, remembereth her service to your Ladyship. So recommending you to the rich grace of Christ, I rest, your Ladyship's, at all obedience in Christ.

S.R.

60/TO MR J.G.[1]

> *Depression in a cloudy day*
> *Darkness of the times*
> *Christ's infinite grace*

London, 30 January 1646

Reverend and dear brother:

I do esteem nothing out of heaven, and next to a communion with Jesus Christ, more than to be in the hearts and prayers of the saints. I know that he feedeth there among the lilies, till the day break. But I am at a low ebb as to any sensible communion with Christ; yea, as low as any soul can be, and do scarce know where I am; and do now make it a question, if any can go to him, who dwelleth in light inaccessible, through nothing but darkness. Surely, all that come to heaven have a stock in Christ; but I know not where mine is. It cannot be enough for me to believe the salvation of others, and to know Christ to be

[1] James Guthrie

the Honey-comb, the Rose of Sharon, the Paradise and Eden of the saints and first-born written in heaven, and not to see afar the borders of that good land.

But what shall I say? Either this is the Lord making grace a new creation, where there is pure nothing and sinful nothing to work upon; or I am gone. I should count my soul engaged to yourself, and others there with you, if you would but carry to Christ for me a letter of cyphers and nonsense (for I know not how to make language of my condition) only showing that I have need of his love; for I know that many fair and washen ones stand now in white before the throne, who were once as black as I am. If Christ pass his word to wash a sinner, it is less to him than a word to make fair angels of black devils. Only let the art of free grace be engaged. I have no one to become surety, nor doth a Mediator, such as he is in all perfection, need a mediator. But what I need, he knoweth; only, it is his depth of wisdom to let some pass millions of miles over score in debt, that they may stand between the winning and the losing, in need of more than ordinary free grace.

Christ hath been multiplying grace by mercy above these five thousand years; and the later-born heirs have so much greater guiltiness, that Christ hath passed more experiments and multiplied essays of heart-love on others, by misbelieving (after it is past all question, many hundreds of ages) that Christ is the undeniable and now uncontroverted treasurer of multiplied redemptions. So now he is saying, 'The more of the disease there is, the more of the physician's art of grace and tenderness there must be'. Only I know that no sinner can put infinite grace to it,[1] so that the Mediator shall have difficulty, or much ado, to save this or that man. Millions of hells of sinners cannot come near to exhaust infinite grace.

[1] That is, cause infinite grace to be at a loss to know what to do.

61/TO WILLIAM GUTHRIE

Depression under dark trials
Dangers of compliance

St Andrews [undated]

Reverend Brother:

I did not dream of such shortness of breath, and fainting in the way toward our country. I thought that I had no more to do than die in my nest, and bow down my sinful head, and let him put on the crown, and so end. I have suffered much; but this is the thickest darkness, and the straitest step of the way I have yet trodden. I see more suffering yet behind, and, I fear, from the keepers of the vine. Let me obtain of you, that you would press upon the Lord's people that they would stand far off from these merchants of souls who have come in amongst you. If the way revealed in the Word be that way, we then know that these soul-cowpers[1] and traffickers show not the way of salvation.

Alas, alas! poor I am utterly lost, my share of heaven is gone, and my hope is poor; I am perished, and I am cut off from the Lord, if hitherto out of the way! But I dare not judge kind Christ; for, if it may be but permitted (with reverence to his greatness and highness be it spoken), I will, before witnesses, produce his own hand that he said, 'This is the way, walk thou in it'. And he cannot except against his own seal. I profess that I am almost broken and a little sleepy, and would fain put off this body. But this is my infirmity, who would be under the shadow and covert of that Good Land, once[2] to be without the reach and blast of that terrible one. But I am a fool; there is none that can overbid, or take

[1] Jobbers in souls.   [2] Once for all, completely.

my lodging over my head, since Christ hath taken it for me.

Dear brother, help me, and get me the help of their prayers who are with you, in whom is my delight. You are much suspected of intended compliance; I mean, not of you only, but of all the people of God with you. It is but a poor thing, the fulfilling of my joy; but let me obtest all the serious seekers of his face, his secret sealed ones, by the strongest consolations of the Spirit, by the gentleness of Jesus Christ, that Plant of Renown, by your last accounts and appearing before God, when the white throne shall be set up, be not deceived with their fair words. Though my spirit be astonished at the cunning distinctions which are found out in the matters of the Covenant, that help may be had against these men. Yet my heart trembleth to entertain the least thought of joining with those deceivers.

Grace, grace be with you. Amen.

62/TO LADY RALSTON

Duty of preferring to live rather than die
Want of unity in the judgments of the godly

October, 1651

Right Worthy esteemed in your excellent Lord Jesus:

With much desire I have longed to hear how you are, since I heard of your being so near the harbour, as seemed; and now, to my great satisfaction, I am informed of your recovery. As for yourself, I grant, to have entered in at the ports of the mansions of glory had been best by far; but yet to stay a little longer here is much more comfortable to yours. Therefore, Mistress, dearly respected in the Lord, you are even heartily welcome, though to share yet further with Zion in her manifold tribulations. Yea, I believe yourself thinks it no disadvantage, but rather one great addition of honour, to come back and bear his reproach yet more in a world of opposition to him. For (to speak so) it is an advantage that is not to be had in heaven itself; for although the inhabitants of that land agree in one to sing the song of the Lamb's praise and commendation, so it is here-away, and here only, where we have occasion to endure shame and contradiction for his worthy sake.

Considering, therefore, the honour of the cross with the glory of the life to come, the saints are hereby rendered completely happy and honourable. It is much selfishness (as I judge it when I get seen best into the mystery of our Lord's cross) to make post haste to be in the land of rest, when a storm of persecution is rising for Christ; for the sluggard and peevish spirit loves rest upon any terms, though never so dishonourable. It is in effect then, far more honourable to seek conformity to Christ in his cross, than be too precipitate in desiring to be like him in glory, and despise and fly away from his sufferings. We use to say that they are very evil-worthy of the sweet who will not endure the sour. I think Christ's pilgrim weeds[1] (he being a Man of sorrows and griefs) are more honourable than ever it became the like of us to wear; especially considering our poor base descent, whom he will have honoured with conformity to himself.

Woe is me that I and many the like of me within the land look so frowardly on Christ's cross, as though it were not his love-allowance to all his followers! It is plainly our gross ignorance that is the cause thereof. Faith, I grant, would suffer affliction for him with good-will, rather than the least iniquity should be committed; but sense loves no bands. For faith, keeping the sway, puts oft-times the carnal man in bondage, and that occasions strife betwixt the flesh and the spirit. The spirit smells no freedom or deliverance but that

[1] Garments of mourning.

which comes from above. The flesh would aye have deliverance without examination of the terms, or wherefrom it comes. As it is the mark of Christ's sheep that they will hear his voice and will not acknowledge a stranger, so it is the mark of faith that it will only receive orders from heaven.

When he declares his mind for bands, it submits to bands, not replying objections to the contrary; and again, when he says, 'Show yourselves, ye prisoners of hope', it discovers time and way, and obeys to come forth, but not till then. But the flesh maketh ever haste, and the first and nearest ease is aye its best choice. The Lord keep his dear people from wanting of any exercise that is measured out by him to them, now when he hides his face, lest we be turned aside to false gods! And when he shows himself again (as he will assuredly do), we ken our change. It is far safer to dwell a little in faith's prison than in sense's fairest liberty. I see nothing so comfortable an evidence of God's staying into, and healing of, this broken and poor land, than that faithful testimony of his precious servants (and strengthened only by him) against the late and sore defection.

Yet if the Lord had not left us a remnant we had been as Sodom and like to Gomorrah. And exalted be our God, only wise and free in his love, that ever any testimony was given! for the hour of temptation was very dark to all once. But to some he showed much light, and helped them with a little help. Others, also, able and dear to him, he hath letten, as yet, remain under the cloud. But the mystery of his wisdom is so high in this that I profess it may render all flesh humble in the dust, and to glory henceforth in nothing but in his upholding strength and free love.

Always, when his due time comes, he will make his servants see that which they do not now see. But, alas, in the meantime there is no harder matter of our trouble to be looked to than the grievous differences of judgments and affections among the Lord's servants; which I know is much pondered by you. And I trust that all our worthy dear friends will labour to the utmost, according to Christ's command, to have the breach made up again, that Satan get not advantage therethrough; for I think nothing makes more for his ends than the defacing of union amongst the Lord's dear ones. I think it should be amongst our many requests to him 'in whom all the building useth to be fitly framed together in love'; yea, the obtaining of this request were a great advantage to the poor Kirk. And if the Lord take pleasure in us, there is yet hope in Israel concerning this thing. But if not, it is like to prove a probable token, amongst some others, of Christ's taking down his tabernacle in this land; which, if he do, we will have sad days.

But the consideration of his pitiful compassion holds forth ground to believe otherwise; upon which ground it is like that he will give us a door of hope, though he do not give full deliverance yet. For our hope is not perished yet from the Lord, because men and carnal reason say so; for none of these are bands or rules to the Almighty! Yea, Zion's lowest ebb shall be the first step to her rise. I have no other reason to give but 'the zeal of the Lord of hosts will perform (it)' [Is 9. 7].

Tender my respects to your dear husband, who is indeed precious in the account of the honest here, for his faithfulness in the hour of temptation.

63/TO LADY KENMURE

Trials
Deadness of spirit
Danger of false security

St Andrews, 26 May 1658

Madam:

I am ashamed of my long silence to your Ladyship. Your tossings and wanderings are known to him, upon whom you have been cast from the breasts, and who hath been your God of old. The temporal loss of creatures, dear to you here, may be the more easily endured, so that the gain of One 'who only hath immortality' groweth.

There is an universal complaint of deadness of spirit on all that know God. He that writes to you, madam, is as deep in this as any, and is afraid of a strong and hot battle, before time be at a close. But no matter, if the Lord crown all with the victorious triumphing of faith. God teacheth us by terrible things in righteousness. We see many things, but we observe nothing. Our drink is sour, grey hairs are here and there on us. We change many lords and rulers; but the same bondage of soul and body remaineth. We live little by faith, but much by sense, according to the times, and by human policy. The watchmen sleep, and the people perish for lack of knowledge. How can we be enlightened when we turn our back on the sun? And must we not be withered when we leave the fountain? It should be my only desire to be a minister, gifted with the white stone, and the new name written on it.

I judge it were fit (now when tall professors, and when many stars fall from heaven, and God poureth the isle of Great Britain from vessel to vessel, and yet we sit and are settled on our lees), to consider how irrecoverable a woe it is to be under a beguile in the matter of eternity. And what if I, who can have a subscribed testimony of many who shall stand at the right hand of the Judge, shall miss Christ's approving testimony, and be set upon the left hand among the goats [*Matt* 7. 22; 25. 8-12 and 33; *Luke* 13. 25-27]?   There is such a beguile and it befalleth many; and what if it befall me, who have but too much art to cozen my own soul and others with the flourish of ministerial or country holiness!

Dear lady, I am afraid of prevailing security. We watch little (I have mainly relation to myself) we wrestle little. I am like one travelling in the night, who fancies he sees a spirit, and is filled with alarm, and dares not tell it to his fellow for fear of increasing his own fear. However, I am sure, when the Master is nigh his coming, it were safe to write over a double and a new copy of our accounts, of the sins of nature, child-hood, youth, riper years, and old age. What if Christ have another written representation of me than I have of myself? Sure his is right; and if it contradict my mistaken and sinfully erroneous account of myself, ah! where am I then? But, madam, I discourage none; I know Christ hath made a new marriage-contract of love, and sealed it with his blood, and the trembling believer shall not be confounded. Grace be with you.

64/TO JAMES DURHAM

[*Written some few days before Durham's death*]

Man's ways not God's ways

St Andrews, 15 June 1658

Sir:

I would ere now have written to you, had I not known that your health, weaker and weaker, could scarce permit you to hear or read. I need not speak much. The Way you know, and have preached to others the skill of the Guide, and the glory of the home beyond death. And when he saith, 'Come and see', it will be your gain to obey and go out and meet the Bridegroom.

What accession is made to the higher house of his kingdom should not be our loss, though it be real loss to the Church of God. But we count one way and the Lord counteth another way. He is infallible, and the only wise God, and needeth none of us. Had he needed the staying in the body of Moses and the prophets he could have taken another way. Who dare bid you cast your thoughts back on wife or children when he hath said, 'Leave them to me, and come up hither'? Or who can persuade you to die or live, as if that were arbitrary to us, and not his alone who hath determined the number of your months? If so it seem good to him, follow your Forerunner and Guide. It is an unknown land to you, who were never there before, but the land is good and the company before the throne desirable, and he who sitteth on the throne is alone a sufficient heaven.

Grace, grace be with you.

65/TO JAMES GUTHRIE, ROBERT TRAILL, AND OTHER
BRETHREN IMPRISONED IN THE CASTLE OF EDINBURGH

On suffering for Christ
God's presence ever with his people
Firmness and constancy required

St Andrews, 1660

Reverend, very dear, and now much honoured Prisoners for Christ:

I am, as to the point of light, at the utmost of persuasion in that kind that it is the cause of Christ which you now suffer for, and not men's interest. If it be for men, let us leave it; but if we plead for God, our own personal safety and man's deliverance will not be peace.

There is a salvation called 'the salvation of God', which is cleanly, pure, spiritual, unmixed, near to the holy Word of God. It is that which we would seek, even the favour of God that he beareth to his people; not simple gladness, but the gladness and goodness of the Lord's chosen. And sure, though I be the weakest of his witnesses, and unworthy to be among the meanest of them, and am afraid that the cause be hurt (though it cannot be lost) by my unbelieving faintness, I would not desire a deliverance separated from the deliverance of the Lord's cause and people. It is enough to me to sing when Zion singeth; and to triumph when Christ triumpheth. I should judge it an unhappy joy to rejoice when Zion sigheth. 'Not one hoof' will be your peace [*Exod* 10. 26]. If Christ doth own me, let me be in the grave in a bloody winding-sheet, and go from the scaffold in four quarters, to grave or no grave. I am his debtor, to seal with sufferings this precious truth. But oh! when it cometh to the push, I dare say nothing, considering my weakness, wickedness and faintness. But fear not you.

You are not, you shall not be alone, the Father is with you. It was not an unseasonable, but a seasonable and necessary duty you were about. Fear him who is Sovereign. Christ is Captain of the castle, and Lord of the keys. The cooling well-spring, and refreshment from the promises, are more than the frownings of the furnace.

I see snares and temptations in capitulating, composing, ceding, minching[1] with distinctions of circumstances, formalities, compliments and extenuations in the cause of Christ. 'A long spoon: the broth is hell-hot.' Hold a distance from carnal compositions, and much nearness to the Fountain, to the favour and refreshing light from the Father of lights speaking in his oracles. This is sound health and salvation. Angels, men, Zion's elders, eye us; but what of all these? Christ is by us, and looketh on us, and writeth up all. Let us pray more, and look less to men. Remember me to Mr Scott and to all the rest. Blessings be upon the head of such as are separated from their brethren. Joseph is a fruitful bough by a well. Grace be with you.

Your loving brother and companion in the kingdom and patience of Jesus Christ.

S.R.

[1] Cutting into small pieces.

66/TO MISTRESS CRAIG

[*On the death of her son*[1]]

Nine reasons for resignation

St Andrews, 4 August 1660

Mistress:

You have so learned Christ, as now (in the furnace) what dross, what shining of faith may appear, must come forth. I heard of the removal of your son Mr Thomas. Though I be dull enough in discerning, yet I was witness to some spiritual savouriness of the new-birth and hope of the resurrection, which I saw in the hopeful youth, when he was, as was feared, a–dying in this city. And since it was written and advisedly appointed, in the spotless and holy decree of the Lord, where, and before what witnesses, and in what manner, whether by a fever, the mother being at the bed, or by some other way in a far country (dear patriarchs died in Egypt, precious to the Lord, and have wanted burials, *Psalm* 79. 3), your safest course will be, to be silent, and command the heart to utter no repining and fretting thoughts of the holy dispensation of God.

1. Beyond the hazard of dispute, the precious youth is perfected and glorified.

2. Had the youth lain year and day, pained beside a witnessing mother, it had been pain and grief lengthened out to you in many portions, and every parcel would have been a little death. Now his holy Majesty hath, in one lump and mass, brought to your ears the news, and hath not divided the grief into many portions.

3. It was not yesterday's thought, nor the other year's

[1] He was drowned while bathing in a river in France.

statute; but a counsel of the Lord of old; and, 'Who can teach the Almighty knowledge?'

4. There is no way of quieting the mind, and of silencing the heart of a mother, but godly submission. The readiest way for peace and consolation to clay-vessels is, that it is a stroke of the Potter and Former of all things. And since the holy Lord hath loosed the grip, when it was fastened sure on your part, I know that your light, and I hope that your heart also, will yield. It is not safe to be pulling and drawing with the omnipotent Lord. Let the pull go with him, for he is strong; and say, 'Thy will be done on earth, as it is in heaven'.

5. His holy method and order is to be adored; sometimes the husband before the wife, and sometimes the son before the mother. So hath the only wise God ordered: and when he is sent before and not lost, in all things give thanks.

6. Meditate not too much on the sad circumstances; the mother was not witness to the last sight; possibly cannot get leave to wind the son, nor to weep over his grave; and he was in a strange land. There is a like nearness to heaven out of all the countries of the earth.

7. This did not spring out of the dust. Feed and grow fat by this medicine and fare of the only wise Lord. It is the art and the skill of faith to read what the Lord writeth upon the cross, and to spell and construct right his sense. Often we miscall words and sentences of the cross, and either put nonsense on his rods, or burden his Majesty with slanders and mistakes, when he mindeth for us thoughts of peace and love, even to do us good in the latter end.

8. It is but a private stroke on a family, and little to the public arrows shot against grieved Joseph, and the afflicted, but ah! dead, senseless and guilty people of God. This is the day of Jacob's trouble.

9. There is a bad way of wilful swallowing of a temptation, and not digesting it, or laying it out of memory without

any victoriousness of faith. The Lord, who forbiddeth fainting, forbiddeth also despising. But it is easier to counsel than to suffer: the only wise Lord furnish patience!

It were not amiss to call home the other youth. I am not a little afflicted for my Lady Kenmure's condition. I desire, when you see her, remember my humble respects to her. My wife heartily remembereth her to you, and is wounded much in mind with your present condition, and suffereth with you. Grace be with you.

67/TO JAMES GUTHRIE[1]

Steadfastness under persecution
The blessedness of martyrdom

St Andrews, 15 February 1661

Dear Brother:

We are very oft comforted with the word of promise; though we stumble not a little at the work of holy providence, some earthly men flourishing as a green herb, and the people of God counted as sheep for the slaughter, and killed all the day long. And yet both word of promise, and work of Providence, are from him whose ways are equal, straight, holy, and spotless.

As for me, when I think of God's dispensations, he might justly have brought to the market-cross, and to the light, my unseen and secret abominations, which would have been no small reproach to the holy name and precious truths of Christ.

---

[1] James Guthrie, with other ministers of the Word, was imprisoned in Edinburgh Castle in the late summer of 1660. He was hanged at the cross of the City on 1 June, 1661. His head was thereafter cut off and fixed on the Nether Bow.

But in mercy he hath covered these, and shapen and carved out more honourable causes of suffering, of which we are unworthy.

And now, dear brother, much dependeth upon the way and manner of suffering; especially, that his precious truths be owned, with all heavenly boldness; and a reason of our hope given in meekness and fear: and the royal crown, and absolute supremacy of our Lord Jesus Christ, the Prince of the kings of the earth, avouched as becometh. For certain it is that Christ will reign, the Father's King in Mount Zion; and his sworn covenant will not be buried. It is not denied that our practical breach of covenant first, and then our legal breach thereof by enacting the same mischief and framing it into a law, may heavily provoke our sweetest Lord. Yet there are a few names in the land that have not defiled their garments, and a holy seed on whom the Lord will have mercy, like the four or five olive-berries upon the top of the shaken olive-tree [*Is* 17. 6], and their eye shall be toward the Lord their Maker.

Think it not strange that men devise against you; whether it be to exile, the earth is the Lord's; or perpetual imprisonment, the Lord is your light and liberty; or a violent and public death, for the kingdom of heaven consisteth in a fair company of glorified martyrs and witnesses, of whom Jesus Christ is the chief witness, who for that cause was born, and came into the world. Happy are you, if you give testimony to the world of your preferring Jesus Christ to all powers. And the Lord will make the innocency and Christian loyalty of his defamed and despised witnesses in this land to shine to after-generations, and will take the Man-Child up to God and to his throne, and prepare a hiding-place in the wilderness for the mother, and cause the earth to help the woman.

Be not terrified; fret not. Forgive your enemies: bless and curse not. For though both you and I should be silent, sad and heavy is the judgment and indignation of the Lord that is abiding the unfaithful watchmen of the Church of Scotland.

The souls under the altar are crying for justice, and there is an answer returned already: the Lord's salvation will not tarry. Cast the burden of wife and children on the Lord Christ; he careth for you and them. Your blood is precious in his sight. The everlasting consolations of the Lord bear you up and give you hope: for your salvation (if not deliverance) is concluded.

Your own brother,

S.R.

68/MR ROBERT CAMPBELL

Steadfastness in protest against Prelacy and Popery

[Undated: Rutherford died on the 20 March 1661, shortly after this letter was written]

Reverend and dear Brother:

You know that this is a time in which all men almost seek their own things and not the things of Jesus Christ. You are alone, as a beacon on the top of a mountain. But faint not; Christ is a numerous multitude himself, yea, millions. Though all the nations were convened against him round about, yet doubt not but he will, at last, arise for the cry of the poor and needy.

For me, I am now near to eternity; and for ten thousand worlds I dare not venture to pass from the protestation against the corruptions of the time, nor go along with the shameless apostasy of the many silent and dumb watchmen of Scotland. But I think it my last duty to enter a protestation in heaven before the righteous Judge, against the practical and legal breach of the Covenant, and all oaths imposed on the consciences of the Lord's people, and all popish, superstitious, and idolatrous mandates of men. Know that the overthrow of the sworn Reformation, the introducing of Popery and the mystery of iniquity, is now set on foot in the three kingdoms; and whosoever would keep their garments clean are under that command, 'Touch not, taste not, handle not'.

The Lord calleth you, dear brother, to be still 'steadfast, unmoveable, and abounding in the work of the Lord'. Our royal kingly Master is upon his journey, and will come, and will not tarry. And blessed is the servant who shall be found watching when he cometh. Fear not men, for the Lord is your light and salvation. It is true, it is somewhat sad and comfortless that ye are alone. But so it was with our precious Master; nor are you alone, for the Father is with you. It is possible that I shall not be an eyewitness to it in the flesh, but I believe he cometh quickly who will remove our darkness, and shine gloriously in the Isle of Britain, as a crowned King, either in a formally sworn covenant, or in his own glorious way; which I leave to the determination of his infinite wisdom and goodness. And this is the hope and confidence of a dying man who is longing and fainting for the salvation of God.

Beware of the ensnaring bonds and obligations, by any hand-writ or otherwise, to give unlimited obedience to any authority, but only in the Lord. For all innocent self-defence (which is according to the Covenant, the Word of God, and the laudable example of the Reformed Churches) is now intended to be utterly subverted and condemned. And what is taken from Christ, as the flower of his prerogative-royal, is now put upon the head of a mortal power; which must be that great idol of indignation that provoketh the eyes of his glory.

Dear brother, let us mind the rich promises that are made to those that overcome, knowing that those that endure to the end shall be saved.

69/TO BRETHREN IN ABERDEEN

Sinful comformity and schismatic designs reproved

St Andrews [undated]

Reverend and dearly Beloved in the Lord:

Grace be to you and peace from God our Father and from the Lord Jesus Christ. There were some who rendered thanks with knees bowed to him 'of whom is named the whole family in heaven and earth', when they heard of 'your work of faith and labour of love and patience of hope in our Lord Jesus', and rejoiced not a little, that where Christ was scarce named in savouriness and power of the Gospel, even in Aberdeen, there Christ hath a few names precious to him, who shall walk with him in white. We looked on it (he knoweth whom we desire to serve in our spirit in the Gospel of his Son) as a part of the fulfilling of that, 'The wilderness and solitary place shall be glad for them; and the desert shall rejoice, and blossom as the rose' [Is 35. 1]. But now it is more grievous to us than a thousand deaths, when we hear that you are shaken and so soon removed from that which you once acknowledged to be the way of God.

Dearly beloved, the sheep follow Christ, who calleth them by name: a stranger will they not follow, but they flee from him, for they know not the voice of a stranger. You know the way, by which you were sealed to the day of redemption; and you received the Spirit by the hearing of faith. Part not with that way, except you see there be no rest for your souls therein. Neither listen to them that say, 'Many were converted under episcopal as well as under presbyterial government, and yet the godly gave testimony against bishops'; for the instruments of conversion loathed Episcopacy, with the ceremonies thereof, and never sealed it with their sufferings. We shall desire instances of any engaged by oaths, and sufferings of the faithful messengers of God, and the manifestations of the Lord's presence, in the way you now forsake, who yet turned from it, and went one step toward sinful separation (and did it in that way ye now aim at) and did yet flourish and grow in grace. But we can bring proofs of many who left it, and went further on to abominable ways of error. And you have it not in your power where you shall lodge at night, having once left the way of God. And many, we know, lost peace and communion with God, and fell into a condition ot withering, and not being able to find their lovers, were forced to return to their first Husband.

We shall entreat you, consider what a stumbling it is to malignant opposers of the way and cause of God (who with their ears heard you, and with their eyes saw you, so strenuously take part with the godly in their sufferings, and profess yourselves for religion, truth, doctrine, government of the house of God, his Covenant and cause) if now you build again what you once destroyed, and destroy what you builded. And shall you not make yourselves, by so doing, transgressors? How shall it wound the hearts of the godly, stain the profession, darken the glory of the Gospel, shake the faith of many, weaken the hands of all, if you (and you first of all in this kingdom) shall stretch out the hand to raze the walls of our Jerusalem, by reason of which the Lord made her 'terrible as an army with banners'! For when the kings came and saw the palaces and bulwarks thereof, they marvelled and were troubled, and hasted away; fear took hold upon them there, and pain as of a woman in travail. And we shall be grieved if you should be heirs to the guiltiness of breaking down the same hedge of the vineyard, for the which the sad indignation of God pursueth this day the Royal Family, many Nobles, houses great and fair, and all the Prelatical party in these three kingdoms.

And when your dear brethren are weak and fainting, shall we believe that you will leave us, and be divided from this so blessed a conjunction? The Lord Jesus Christ, we trust, shall walk in the midst of the golden candlesticks, and be with us, if you will be gone from us. Beloved in the Lord, we cannot but be persuaded better things of you; and we shall not conceal from you that we are ignorant what to answer when we are reproved, on your behalf, in regard that your change to another gospel-way (which the Lord avert!) is so much the more scandalous, that the sudden alteration (unknown to us before) now overtaketh you when men come amongst you against whom the furrows of the fields of Scotland do complain. Forget not, dear brethren, that Christ hath now the fan in his hand, and this is also the day of the Lord that shall burn as an oven, and that Christ now sitteth as a refiner of silver, purifying the sons of Levi, and purging them as gold and silver, that they may offer unto the Lord an offering in righteousness; and those that keep the word of his (not their own) patience shall be delivered from the hour of temptation that shall come on all the earth to try them.

If you exclude all non-converts from the visible city of God (in which daily, multitudes in Scotland, in all the four quarters of the land, above whatever our fathers saw, throng into Christ), shall they not be left to the lions and wild beasts of the forest, even to Jesuits, seminary priests, and other seducers? For the magistrate hath no power to compel them to hear the Gospel, nor have you any church-power over them, as you teach; and they bring not love to the Gospel and to Christ out of the womb with them; and so they must be left to embrace what religion is most suitable to corrupt nature.

Nor can it be a way approven by the Lord in Scripture, to excommunicate from the visible church (which is the office-house of the free grace of God, and his draw-net) all the multitudes of non-converts, baptized and visibly within the covenant of grace, which are in Great Britain, and all the Reformed Churches; and so to shut the gates of the Lord's gracious calling upon all these (because they are not, in your judgment, chosen to salvation), when once you are within yourselves.[1] For how can the Lord call Egypt his people, and Assyria the work of his hands, and all the Gentiles (who for numbers are as the flocks of Kedar, and the abundance of the sea) the kingdom of our Lord and of his Christ, if you number infants (as many do), and all such as your charity cannot judge converts (as others do) among heathens and pagans, who have not a visible claim and interest in Christ? The candlestick is not yours, nor the house; but Christ fixeth and removeth the one, and buildeth or casteth down the other, according to his sovereignty.

We in humility judge ourselves, though the chief of sinners, the sons of Zion and of the seed of Christ. If you remove from us, and carry from hence the candlestick, let our Father be judge, and show us why the Lord hath bidden you come out from among us. We look upon this visible church, though black and spotted, as the hospital and guest-house of sick, halt, maimed and withered over which Christ is Lord, Physician and Master. And we would wait upon those who are not yet in Christ as our Lord waited upon us and you both. We, therefore, your brethren, children of one Father, cannot but with tears and exceeding sorrow of heart earnestly entreat, beseech, and obtest you, by the love of our Lord Jesus Christ, by his sufferings and precious ransom which he paid for us both, by the consolations of his Spirit, by your appearance before the dreadful tribunal of our Lord Jesus, yea, and charge you before God and the same Lord Jesus, 'who shall judge the quick and the dead at his appearing and His Kingdom'; break not the spirits and hearts of those to whom you are dear as their own soul. Forsake not the assemblies of the people of God; let us not divide.

[1] That is, when you yourselves have got safe within.

Not a few of the people of God in this shire of Fife (in whose name I now write) dare say, if you depart, that you will leave Christ behind you with us, and the golden candlesticks; and shut yourselves, we much fear, out of the hearts and prayers of thousands dear to Jesus Christ in Scotland. Therefore, before you fix judgment and practice on any untrodden path, let a day of humiliation be agreed upon by us all, and our Father's mind and will inquired, through our one common Saviour. And let us see one another's faces at best conveniency, and plead the interest of Christ, and be comforted; and not be stumbled at your ways.

So expecting your answer, we shall pray that the God of peace, who brought again from the dead our Lord Jesus, that great Shepherd of the sheep, through the blood of the everlasting covenant, may make you perfect in every work to do his will, working in you that which is well-pleasing in his sight through Jesus Christ

BRIEF NOTES ON RUTHERFORD'S
CORRESPONDENTS

ABERDEEN: Brethren in Aberdeen would be well known to Rutherford in view of his residence in their City as an exile for eighteen months (1636-38).

ANWOTH PARISHIONERS: Rutherford was their minister from 1627 until 1638.

BAUTIE, JAMES: Seems to have been preparing for the Presbyterian ministry when Rutherford wrote to him. After ordination he ministered in Co. Down, N. Ireland. On refusal to take the oath of fidelity to the Commonwealth in 1650 he was banished from the kingdom. His later history is unknown.

BLAIR, ROBERT: Born at Irvine in 1593. He became Presbyterian minister at Bangor, N. Ireland in 1623. Anglican prelates opposed him and secured his dismissal in 1634. He embarked with other ministers for New England but storms compelled them to return. In 1638 he became minister at Ayr but soon moved to St Andrews, where he and Rutherford became firm friends. He lived till 1666.

BOYD, LADY (nee Christina Hamilton): Eldest daughter of 1st Earl of Haddington. The 6th Lord Boyd (d. 1628) was her second husband. She was noted for her exemplary Christian life and character ('grave, diligent, prudent'). At her death the whole Scottish Parliament, then sitting at St. Andrews, rose out of respect and attended her funeral.

CALLY, LAIRD OF (John Lennox): Cally is near Anwoth. Little is known of him.

CARDONESS, LADY; CARDONESS, the ELDER; CARDONESS, the YOUNGER: Cardoness the Elder (John Gordon) lived in Cardoness Castle in the parish of Anwoth. He was a descendant of Gordon of Lochinvar and prominent in local parochial affairs. Little is known of

Cardoness the Younger except that he took part in the Civil War in England. We gather from the Letters that human nature was strong in both father and son.

CARLETON, LAIRD OF (John Fullarton): Carleton was in the parish of Borgue, not far from Anwoth.

CASSINCARRIE, LAIRD OF: Cassincarrie was a spot near Anwoth, close to the scene of martyrdom of the two Wigtown martyrs almost 50 years after Rutherford's letter was written.

CLARK, JOHN: Probably a parishioner of Anwoth.

COLVILLE, ALEXANDER: A Presbyterian Elder of Blair in the parish of Carnock, Fifeshire. He held high legal office and befriended Rutherford when he appeared before the Court of High Commission in 1630. He was a prominent member of the Scottish Presbyterian church for a lengthy period.

CORBET, THOMAS: A parishioner of Anwoth.

CRAIG, MISTRESS: Nothing is known of this lady.

CRAIGHILL, LADY; CRAIGHILL, LORD: Sir John Hope (created Lord Craighill) was the most eminent Scottish lawyer of his day. He sympathised with persecuted ministers and helped in their defence. He became a Lord of Session in 1632 and later, President of the Court. In 1645 he became a member of the Privy Council.

CULROSS, LADY (nee Elizabeth Melville): Her father was a Privy Councillor to James VI of Scotland (later James I of England). She was an eminent Christian lady: 'The more she enjoyed access to God, therein she hungered the more'. She was present at the famous Communion season at Shotts (June, 1630) when some five hundred were converted under the preaching of John Livingstone.

CUNNINGHAM, ROBERT: An eminent minister of the gospel at Holywood, N. Ireland. In 1636 he and others were driven out of Ireland by Prelatists. He settled at Irvine (Ayrshire). He died in March, 1637, scarcely eight months after Rutherford wrote to him.

DALGLEISH, WILLIAM: A faithful and much-blessed minister of the Word for the conjoint parishes of Anwoth, Kirkdale, and Kirkmabreck. When Rutherford began his ministry, Anwoth became a 'distinct parochial charge'. In 1635 Dalgleish was relieved of his position on account of his anti-episcopal testimony, but returned in 1637 when the strong reaction against episcopacy set in. After Rutherford's death he was again evicted for nonconformity.

DICKSON, DAVID (1583-1662): Professor of Philosophy in the University of Glasgow, 1610-18. In 1618 he became minister of Irvine but in 1622 was banished by the episcopalians to Turriff in Aberdeenshire. He returned to Irvine after a year and was prominent in the famous Stewarton Revival, 1623-30. He took a leading part in promoting the National Covenant of 1638. In 1642 he became Professor of Divinity in the University of Glasgow. Later he held a similar office in the University of Edinburgh. He published several commentaries, including one on the Psalms.

DURHAM, JAMES (1622-58): Minister of Blackfriars Church, Glasgow, from 1647. He died in 1658 at the age of 35, only ten days after Rutherford's letter was written to him. He is famed for his writings, which include Expositions of Job, the Song of Solomon, and the Book of Revelation.

EARLSTON, the ELDER and YOUNGER (Alexander Gordon): Descendants of the house of Gordon of Lochinvar, which was influenced by the teachings of John Wycliffe. The house of Earlston was located near Carsphairn in the inland parts of Kirkcudbright. Alexander Gordon was a staunch Presbyterian who appeared before the Court of High Commission in defence of his principles (1635). He was fined heavily. He later represented Galloway in the Scottish Parliament. His eldest son, who inherited the family estate in 1655, was killed in 1679 while assisting the Covenanting cause.

ELLIS, FULK: Lived at Carrickfergus, N. Ireland, and followed the military profession. A zealous Covenanter, he joined the Scots in resisting Charles I in the Bishops' War of 1640. He returned to Ireland later but seems to have been killed in action in 1643.

FLEMING, JOHN: Bailie of Leith. He was a timber merchant who befriended Rutherford in days of need and supplied him with necessities.

GAITGIRTH, LADY (nee Isabel Blair): She married James Chalmers (of Gaitgirth, near Monkton, Ayrshire), a man prominent in the Covenanting cause during the 1630s and 1640s.

GLENDINNING, WILLIAM: Son of Robert Glendinning, minister of Kirkcudbright. He became Provost of Kirkcudbright. Persecuted by the Bishop of Galloway he became a zealous Covenanter. During the 1640s he was prominent in the Scottish Presbyterian cause.

GORDON, ALEXANDER (of Earlston): See Earlston.

GORDON, JOHN (of Cardoness): Elder and Younger (see Cardoness).

GORDON, JOHN (of Rusco): The Laird of Rusco Castle, two miles from Anwoth.

GORDON, ROBERT (of Knockbreck): 'A single-hearted and painful Christian much employed at parliaments and public meetings after the year 1638.' Knockbreck is in the parish of Borgue, which adjoins Anwoth and overlooks Wigtown Bay.

GORDON, WILLIAM (of Whitepark): Little, if anything, is known of this man. Whitepark was an estate near Castle Douglas, some 15 miles from Anwoth.

GORDON, WILLIAM (of Kenmure): Nothing is known of this person.

GUTHRIE, JAMES (1612?-61): The son of the Laird of Guthrie, Forfarshire. It was under the influence of Rutherford that Guthrie, hitherto an episcopalian, became a Presbyterian and Covenanter. He became minister at Stirling in 1649. Prominent in all national affairs in the 1640s and 1650s, he incurred the hatred of the royalist party and in 1660 he was imprisoned in Edinburgh Castle. He was charged with 'high treason' and sent to the scaffold in June, 1661. His head was fixed on the Nether Bow. To his friends he was known as Sickerfoot. His steadfastness inspired the covenanting party to resist the episcopalians.

GUTHRIE, WILLIAM (1620-65): Son of the Laird of Pitforthy, Forfarshire, and cousin to James Guthrie. He owed his conversion to the ministry of Rutherford at St Andrews. In 1644 he became minister of Fenwick, Nr Kilmarnock. He is chiefly remembered as the author of *The Christian's Great Interest*, first published in 1658.

HAMILTON, JAMES: Minister of the gospel in Co. Down, N. Ireland. Under persecution he left for New England, but storms forced him to return. He became minister at Dumfries and later at Edinburgh. A man 'bold for truth'.

HENDERSON, ALEXANDER (1583-1646): An episcopalian who, after conversion, became a presbyterian and a prominent leader in the opposition to prelacy. He was a member of the Westminster Assembly of Divines, and described as 'the fairest ornament after Mr John Knox that ever the Church of Scotland did enjoy'.

HENDERSON, JOHN (of Rusco): A parishioner who farmed the 'home-steading' of Rusco (Anwoth).

KILMALCOLM, PARISHIONERS OF: Kilmalcolm was a rural parish, near Greenock in Renfrewshire. It seems to have been distinguished for its godliness.

KENMURE, LADY: Jane Campbell, Viscountess of Kenmure: daughter of the 7th Earl of Argyle. In 1628 she married John Gordon of Lochinvar, afterwards Viscount Kenmure. His untimely death, after a notable deathbed repentance, occurred in 1634. She married again in 1640, but a second widowhood shortly commenced. In 1661 her brother (the 8th Earl of Argyle) was executed for 'high treason' after a life of political activity. She lived into the 1670s after what appears to have been an exemplary Christian life.

KENNEDY, JOHN: Bailie of Ayr. An eminent Christian, prominent in public affairs during the 1640s.

KILCONQUHAR, LADY: Wife of Sir John Carstairs of Kilconquhar in Fifeshire. (Bonar records that the local pronunciation is Kinneucher).

LEIGHTON, DR ALEXANDER: A native of Forfarshire. He was both a minister of the Word and a practising physician. A zealous Presbyterian incensed by Laud's innovations, he published *Zion's Plea against Prelacy* in 1628. The Star Chamber thereupon sentenced him to branding on the face (with letters S.S.: Sower of Sedition), to a fine of £10,000, to the pillory, to whipping, to have his ears cut off and his nose slit, and thereafter to life imprisonment. After ten years he was released from prison by the Long Parliament. At the same time his fine was cancelled and £6,000 was voted to him as compensation for the ill-treatment which he had received. One of his sons was the famous Robert Leighton, Archbishop of Glasgow, and author of a famous commentary on I Peter.

LINDSAY, JAMES: Unknown.

LIVINGSTONE, WILLIAM: Probably an Anwoth parishioner.

MACMILLAN, JEAN: Probably an Anwoth parishioner.

M'KAIL, HUGH: Minister of Irvine, Ayrshire.

M'NAUGHT, MARION: Daughter of the Laird of Kilquhanatie of Kirk-patrick Durham (near Castle Douglas), Kirkcudbright. Also connected through her mother with the House of Kenmure. She married William Fullarton, Provost of Kirkcudbright, and is noted for her 'rare godliness and public spirit'. She had three children—Grizel, Samuel and William. She died in 1643 at the age of 58. Forty-five letters written to her by Rutherford are preserved. She was his favourite correspondent.

MOWAT, MATTHEW: Son of the Laird of Busbie and minister at Kilmarnock. One of the leading ministers of West Scotland. Rutherford held him in high esteem.

RALSTON, LADY: Wife of William Ralston of Renfrewshire. She was a person of 'distinguished piety'.

STUART, JOHN: Provost of Ayr. 'A godly and zealous Christian of long standing and from his earliest years.' He used his worldly goods to relieve the oppressed. He was among those who endeavoured unsuccessfully to emigrate to New England.

STUART, ROBERT: Probably the son of Provost Stuart of Ayr.

TRAILL, ROBERT (1603-78): A zealous Covenanter, minister of Grey-friars, Edinburgh, from 1648. When Charles II came to the throne in 1660 he joined James Guthrie and others in reminding the king of his obligation to keep the Covenant. For this he was driven into exile in Holland. His son (also Robert) became a presbyterian minister in Kent and produced a number of evangelical treatises.

WILSON, JAMES: The identity of this person is a matter of conjecture. He may have been a minister at Inch (Stranraer) or at Dysart (Fifeshire).

AN OUTLINE OF RUTHERFORD'S LIFE

1600   Approximate date of birth in Nisbet parish, Roxburgh-shire (early education probably at Jedburgh).

1617   Entered University of Edinburgh.

1621   Graduated M.A.

1623-6   Regent of Humanity at Edinburgh University.

1626   'Became seriously religious' about this time.

1627   Appointed to Parish of Anwoth (Galloway).

1630   Involved in law case before Court of High Commission, as he refused obedience to the Articles of Perth.

Death of wife (nee Eupham Hamilton).

1636   Published Treatise against Arminianism (*Exercitationes Apologeticae pro Divina Gratia*).

1636   Bishop of Galloway got Court of High Commission to forbid him to exercise his ministry. 'Exiled' to Aberdeen from August, 1636.

(This inaugurates the 'Letter-writing Period' of his life.)

1638   The Scottish nation, in revolt against Laudian Episcopacy, signed the NATIONAL COVENANT.

Rutherford returned to Anwoth.

1638   The Glasgow Assembly appointed him Professor of Divinity at St Mary's College, St Andrews. He reluctantly accepted.

Attended several Covenanting Assemblies.

Married Jean M'Math.

1642   Published *Plea for Presbytery* (against Independency).

1643-47   An active member of the Westminster Assembly of Divines (November, 1643-November, 1647). Resident in London.

	1644: Published *Lex Rex* (a political treatise) and *Due Right of Presbyteries*.
	1645: Published *Trial and Triumph of Faith*.
	1646: Published *Divine Right of Church Government*.
	1647: Published *Christ dying and drawing sinners to Himself*.
1648	Resumed duties at St Andrews. Became Principal of St Mary's College.
	Published several minor works.
1651	Appointed Rector of University of St Andrews.
	Published *De Divina Providentia*.
1650–61	Active in Scottish national affairs.
1655	Published *The Covenant of Life Opened*.
1659	Published *Influences of the Life of Grace*.
1660	(After Restoration of Charles II). Deprived of all offices and summoned to appear before Parliament on a charge of treason.
	Too ill to make the journey.
1661	(March) Death of Rutherford.
	(1664: First edition of *Letters* published.)
	(1668: His MS. *Examen Arminianismi* published in Holland.)
	(His widow and daughter Agnes survived him: all the children of his first marriage and six of the second predeceased him.)